Blake, Coleridge, Wordsworth, Lamb, Etc.

Henry Crabb Robinson, Edith Julia Morley

BIBLIOLIFE

HENRY CRABB ROBINSON
(*ætat* 86)
*After the engraving by W. Holl, from a photograph by
Maull & Co.*

BLAKE,
COLERIDGE, WORDSWORTH,
LAMB, *ETC.*

being

Selections from the Remains

of

HENRY CRABB ROBINSON

Edited by

EDITH J. MORLEY

1922

Manchester ، ، ، ، At The University Press
London, New York, &c. ، Longmans, Green & Co.

" Of studie took he moost cure and moost heede,
Not o word spak he moore than was neede,
And that was seyd in forme and reuerence,
And short and quyk and ful of hy sentence.
Sownynge in moral vertu was his speche,
And gladly wolde he lerne and gladly teche."

CONTENTS

CONTENTS

ILLUSTRATIONS

PREFATORY NOTE

THIS small volume of selections is the first-fruits of my work at the *Remains* of Crabb Robinson, preserved in Dr. Williams's Library: on this I have been engaged, with interruptions due to the war, since 1912. My intention is ultimately to publish all the correspondence and all those parts of the *Diary* and *Reminiscences* which are of interest from the standpoint of literary history. The task is a lengthy one, and meanwhile, since Sadler's edition, originally published in 1869, though in some respects excellent, has long been out-of-print, and is, moreover, badly-proportioned and unreliable, it is thought that a selection from the large mass of available material may prove welcome to many readers. The *Blake Reminiscences* were put together by Crabb Robinson in 1825: they are to be found at the end of the first volume of the *Reminiscences* which were compiled by him from the journals and from memory between 1845 and 1853. Many, but not all, of the passages relating to Blake have already been printed in Gilchrist's *Life*, and elsewhere. I have reprinted only those which are not found substantially in the extracts from H. C. R.'s letters and from his *Diary*, which are here given the preference since they have the interest of contemporary impressions, as distinct from the later less vivid criticism.

The early part of the *Diary* is full of references to the great writers of the first quarter of the nineteenth century, and especially to Wordsworth, Coleridge, and Lamb, with whom H. C. R. was in close personal intercourse. Many such passages are known from Sadler's volumes, but H. C. R.'s own selections from his many memories of them have not hitherto been printed. These *Reminiscences* extend from the year 1808 to 1829, and were penned in his old age between 1849 and 1853. These, too, are supplemented, and in some cases, where the accounts overlap, replaced, first by Crabb Robinson's references to Coleridge's lectures in both his *Diary* and correspondence, (much of this material has not previously been printed,) and secondly by the

PREFATORY NOTE

complete publication for the first time of those parts of the *Diary* and letters which give an account of the quarrel between Wordsworth and Coleridge, and the reconciliation effected between them in 1812 by Crabb Robinson. It was tempting to enlarge the volume by the inclusion of other matter, *e.g.* the *Diary* accounts of Hazlitt's lectures, Carlyle's letters relating to his translations from German novels, or Landor's letters, which are among the contents of outstanding interest. But I have thought it wiser to confine myself to very definite limits, in order that the volume may be within the reach of all those who desire to possess it.

My thanks are due to Dr. Williams's Trustees for their permission to publish these extracts from the MSS., and to the Rev. Travers Herford, their secretary, and Mr. Stephen Jones and Miss Borthwick, his assistants, for the kindness they have shown in facilitating my work at the Library. Mr. Herford is responsible for the transcripts from shorthand, the key to which he has discovered and been good enough to hand on to me. I am also much indebted to Mr. McKechnie, of the Manchester University Press, for his invaluable help in preparing the volume for publication.

Edith J. Morley.

University College, Reading,
  August 1922.

[Words and letters in square brackets have been supplied by the Editor. H. C. R.'s spelling and punctuation have been corrected, and his abbreviations, particularly of proper names, written *in extenso* wherever these alterations seemed to make the text clearer. Apart from such changes, it is an exact transcript from the originals.]

INTRODUCTION

HENRY CRABB ROBINSON

1775-1867

IN the frescoes in the hall at Dr. Williams's Library, Gordon Square, London—the original dining-room of University Hall —Crabb Robinson sits by himself, pen in hand, apparently recalling the many friendships of an exceptionally long life. On the surrounding panels, arranged in four separate groups, are some of the most distinguished of his acquaintances and intimates, English and foreign : among the four-and-thirty thus selected, to name a few of them, are Wordsworth, Coleridge, the Lambs, Blake, Hazlitt, and Landor ; Goethe, Schiller, Wieland, Arndt, Tieck, and Schlegel ; Madame de Staël, Irving, Dr. Arnold, and Robertson. These figures are representative, but they do not in any sense exhaust the tale of his literary friends, still less of his literary experiences. The earliest reference to poetry in his *Reminiscences* is to the publication of *John Gilpin* (1782), for learning which by heart he was given sixpence. The last entry in his *Diary*, five days before his death in 1867, concerns Matthew Arnold's essay on the *Function of Criticism*. Between those dates it is no exaggeration to say that Crabb Robinson read every important work that appeared in English or in German, and that he knew, and often was friendly with, most of their writers.

As a boy he was thrilled by the news that the Bastille had fallen, and his Jacobinism was tempered only by his encounters with French refugees. He sympathized with Horne Tooke, with Hardy and with Thelwall, and was at first an ardent admirer of Godwin, with whom he long remained on friendly terms, though he came to disapprove of both his philosophy and his morals. He lived to be what he called himself in 1832, a " conservative reformer or reforming conservative," while in his old age he read the writings of Gladstone and President Lincoln's inaugural speech.

INTRODUCTION

The boy who saw—he was too far off to hear—John Wesley preach at Colchester in 1790, in 1846 began to be intimate with F.W. Robertson, and was an admirer of Frederick Maurice as well as of Newman. Robinson was a student at the University of Jena in 1800, remaining in Germany for more than five years; he was foreign correspondent of *The Times* in Altona in 1807, and a life-long friend of Walter as a result. In the following year he was " foreign editor," and in this capacity in 1808 escaped from Corunna only just before the battle. His *Diary* records in detail contemporary emotions after Trafalgar and Waterloo; in May 1856 he mentions a " peace sermon " after the Crimea, and there is a detailed account of the Prussian victories of 1866.

Machinery riots and rick burning, the massacre at Peterloo, the first spring bed in which he slept, the first steamers, the first railway [1]—all these things are described and commented upon by this indefatigable diarist; he tells of elections before the Reform Bill, of the long fight for the abolition of slavery, of criminal prosecutions when the death-penalty was inflicted for petty theft, of current prices at various periods, and of social manners and customs. His *Remains* thus serve as a source for various kinds of investigation.

They present, nevertheless, a formidable task to the investigator. Dr. Sadler's edition of the *Diary, Reminiscences*, and *Correspondence*—the only one hitherto available—confessedly does not include more than a twenty-fifth or thirtieth part of the whole. From 1811 to 1867 there is a detailed daily journal; from 1790 to 1843 there are four huge volumes of *Reminiscences*, averaging 450 folio pages; there are 32 volumes of correspondence, each containing some 160 letters—for the most part to or

---

[1] " We hear of some astonishing inventions by means of steam, by which carriages are to be impelled on the public roads to the exclusion of horses."—*Thomas Robinson to H. C. R., Nov.* 22, 1829. On June 10, 1833, H. C. R. travelled by rail from Liverpool to Manchester and back. On July 4 he wrote a detailed description of his experiences to his brother Thomas.

xii

INTRODUCTION

from himself—many of them very long. These range over Robinson's whole life, some of them being family letters of earlier date. In addition there are 28 volumes containing *Journals of Tours*, and various volumes and bundles of miscellanea. We know from the *Diary* that, nevertheless, much time was spent by Robinson towards the end of his life in the destruction of papers and of letters which he thought would prove valueless to posterity. It cannot be claimed that everything which is preserved merits publication. Inevitably, much in so detailed a *Diary* must for us who come after be unprofitable reading. People of importance in their day, or events and discussions which once loomed large, have ceased to be interesting. We do not want to know exactly where Robinson visited and dined on every one of 365 days every year. The part he took as a young man in debates, or later on in law-suits as a practising barrister, or in discussions throughout his life; his services as mediator between his friends, or as adviser and guide to all and sundry; his errors, real and imaginary, of omission and commission—some of this indubitably could be spared with advantage. But the man who emerges from this mass of material is, nevertheless, a lovable personality—no Boswell certainly, but one who possessed a genuine gift for characterization, an instinct for friendship, and the power to stamp himself and his experience with extraordinary vividness on his pages. This is no mere prosy raconteur, unable to distinguish between small things and great; no shorthand reporter taking indiscriminate notes of what passes before his eyes. The man has a mind of his own; he has critical ability and the power to estimate the worth of new works, prose or poetry, good as well as bad. In 1820 he was already hailing Keats as a great poet; he at once recognized the value of Macaulay's history; long before he knew the name of their author he, like the rest of the world, was devouring the *Waverley Novels*, but, unlike most people, with an instinctive preference for the more successful of them. *Kenilworth* and *Ivanhoe*, for example, are recognized as definitely inferior to the *Heart of Midlothian*

INTRODUCTION

and *Rob Roy*. But, above all, it is as the admirer and missionary of Wordsworth among English men of letters that Crabb Robinson is best remembered, and to him and his readings and quotations in early days Wordsworth owed a large proportion of his first audience, fit though few. Moreover, as his German friends recognized, Crabb, for so he was always called by his intimates in later life, was one of the earliest to popularize German literature and to introduce German philosophy into England. The man who, as a student at Jena, had been introduced to Goethe, had heard Schelling lecture upon Methodology, and had successfully impersonated [1] Fichte, never ceased to acclaim, to read, and to write about the first-named, never forgot to sing the praises of Kant, to magnify the Schlegels, and to spread the gospel of transcendentalism. Mme. de Staël owed to him most of the information which resulted in her *De l'Allemagne* : she summoned him to Berlin in 1804—the letter is extant—that he might help her to acquire some notion of German philosophy, and cheerfully acknowledged : " Si vous avez un moment de loisir pour m'écrire quelque chose sur Kant vous augmenteriez mes richesses morales car je n'entends rien qu'à travers vos idées." Later on she told the Duke of Weimar : " J'ai voulu connaître la philosophie allemande ; j'ai frappé à la porte de tout le monde, Robinson seul me l'a ouverte."

Remembering these friendships and these achievements, reading as we may in his *Diary* and letters of Robinson's innumerable acts of kindness, many of which involved not only trouble and self-sacrifice, but also the power to give valuable help in business and in family difficulties, we may as soon believe in Macaulay's strange theory of the " inspired idiot," as in H. C. R.'s own estimate of his character, ability, and influence. He is curiously detached in his self-criticism, as also in his judgments on the criticisms passed upon him by other people. His parents had been known in their youth as " the handsome couple." Their

---

[1] *See* Sadler, vol. i, p. 106 : Visit to Würzburg, 1804.

INTRODUCTION

youngest son cherished no illusions about his own personal appearance. Thus he comments upon Strutt's portrait of him in
1820 : " It has merit and is in some respects a good likeness, but
it caricatures my peculiarities . . . As I dislike my own external
appearance, I was not pleased with this representation of myself
. . . I am . . . offended by the unpleasant expression which, though
not uglier than my own, is ugly in a different way." Similarly
when, in 1829, Goethe sends him to one Schmeller, to have a
portrait taken, he describes this as being "a head in crayons,
frightfully ugly, and very like," or when he sits to Ewing for
his bust, this " has great merit, for it is a strong likeness without
being disgusting." The account of H. C. R.'s ugliness is confirmed from less prejudiced sources, and may therefore be
credited. Thus Bagehot writes of him in his admirable essay
(*Literary Studies*, vol. ii) : " His face was pleasing from its
animation, its kindness, and its shrewdness, but the nose was one
of the most slovenly which nature had ever turned out, and the
chin of excessive length, with portentous power of extension . . .
Mr. Robinson . . . made a very able use of the chin at a conversational crisis, and just at the point of a story pushed it out, and
then very slowly drew it in again, so that you always knew when
to laugh, and the oddity of the gesture helped you in laughing."
Again, Miss Fenwick, Wordsworth's friend, writes to Henry
Taylor, January 26, 1839, that there was " a series of ugliness in
quick succession, one look more ugly than the one which preceded it, particularly when he is asleep. He is always asleep when
he is not talking . . . On which occasions little Willy [Words-
worth's grandson] contemplates him with great interest and often
inquires 'What kind of face has Mr. Robinson ?' ' A very nice
face ' is the constant answer ; then a different look comes, and
another inquiry of, ' What kind of a face was that ?' ' A nice
face too.' What an odd idea he must have of nice faces."

According to his own account H. C. R. was indolent, lacked
concentration, and was a poor lawyer who was incapable of
mastering legal theory, though he often obtained deserved credit

by his speeches. He declared himself never to have remedied the defects of his early education, to have a smattering of many subjects as a result of much desultory reading, but to have no profound knowledge of any one of them. Nor had he literary ability, and he could not write except in a pedestrian way: " Sir," he would reiterate, " I have no literary talent. I cannot write. I never *could* write anything, and I never *would* write anything." " I never knew any law, sir, but I knew the practice." " I am nothing, and never was anything, not even a lawyer." " You see that my memory is quite gone; though that is an absurd way of talking, for I never had any." He had wasted his life, and there was an end of it. The only talent he had ever possessed was for speaking, and even that he had often abused by unduly monopolizing the conversation.

There is, further, a delightful comment when he was going through the papers left by his friend Hamond, whose suicide at the end of 1819 was a great grief to him. " I was interested in a paragraph about myself—not of indiscriminate eulogy, though of friendly appreciation. The unfavourable features of my character are all truly given, and except the epithet *ingenious*, which I disclaim, the other qualities are not given me without foundation." Here is the passage in question: " March 1816. Paris. Miss Williams . . . called H. C. R. an *interesting* man. Now, he is a kind-hearted, gay, ingenious, animated, well-read man, with a good taste in morals, but he is far from being an interesting man . . . His manners are too coarse—he has too little ambition, too much vanity and garrulity." An ordinary individual, we imagine, would scarcely accept such a description of himself as " friendly appreciation," " truly given" if only the one intellectual quality ascribed to him were eliminated.[1] Robinson has too frequently

Cf. *Diary*, June 16, 1820: " M. does not know how liberally I feel on such matters, and I daresay he feels greatly embarrassed by what need not trouble him. His unfavourable opinion of me was founded on my talking too much—he considered me as one of the men who hunt merely after talent without having a sincere

been taken at his own valuation, but it is certain that his self-depreciation and extraordinary modesty do him scant justice. W. S. Landor wrote of him early in their acquaintance, in 1831: " He was a barrister, and notwithstanding, both honest and modest—a character I never heard of before," and this genuine humility is apparent in his estimates of himself. To take two examples as typical of many. His *Diary* is written in a simple, unassuming, direct style which at first may lead the unwary to ignore this narrative power and unusual gift for reporting conversation, and thereby revealing the character of the speakers. He does not understand Blake ; he thinks him indubitably mad. But H. C. R.'s account of his interviews with Blake are the most revealing contemporary interpretations we possess of the mystic poet-painter and his personality. Many people have written well of Lamb, whose lovable self is an inspiration to his critics. But who has said more in a single sentence than H. C. R. has included in the following comment : " Lamb, who needs very little indulgence for himself, is very indulgent towards others " ? (June 15, 1815). What force of judgment there is in all his criticisms, and some of these are adverse, on the character of Wordsworth, whom he worshipped this side idolatry as much as any ; how well he depicts Coleridge in those " innings-for-one that he called conversation." These character sketches—and the *Diary* bristles with them, great men and small, poets, statesmen, revolutionaries, criminals in the dock, lawyers on circuit, judges on the bench, chance acquaintances picked up on the road—these are not mere lucky flukes. " True ease in writing comes from art, not chance," and there is the genuine art, which conceals itself,

---

pursuit of either truth or taste. This he wrote in 1812—but in 1816 he wrote, after coming to town, that he was convinced that I was not a *clever* man—the word 'clever' he had struck out, and softened his remark by substituting the word *first-rate*. I know myself not to be even a second or third-rate man—I also know that I have neither the wit nor [a] great deal of humour which in 1812 he thought I had."

INTRODUCTION

in H. C. R.'s achievements. The statement that he "never *could* write anything" is abundantly disproved on his own evidence.

Similarly with the assertion that he never had any memory. There is no need to go to the testimony of Professor de Morgan [1] or of Bagehot, the friends of his last years, when he might well be excused had his faculties failed him. But once more his oft-repeated complaint is incontrovertibly contradicted by his own writings—even by the least interesting of these, the journals of his tours, or by the reminiscences of his experiences as boy and man. No doubt the daily journal helped him with the latter, but even the *Diary* [2] was not always filled up day by day; sometimes a week's doings were inserted in the small hours after a long day in the courts, and the *Diary* is frequently supplemented thirty years later by incidents it was not considered fitting to include—even in cipher—at the time of their occurrence. To get a complete picture it is often necessary to consult both the first draft and the later, the very much later, working-up.

Crabb Robinson's chief gift was, however, for conversation. Essentially a "clubbable" man, he was, and felt himself to be, pre-eminently at home at the Athenæum, of which he was one of the earliest members and where much of his time was passed, especially as he grew older. But everywhere his sociability and genius for getting on with all sorts and conditions of men and women stood him in good stead. An excellent whist player, he frequented Lamb's parties; he played chess with Mrs. Barbauld,

---

[1] Professor of Mathematics at University College, London. For his account of H. C. R. *see* the Appendix to Dr. Sadler's edition of the *Diary*, etc.

[2] Since the above lines were written I have come across some dozens of small pocket-books in which the events were jotted down which were afterwards elaborated in the *Diary*. In these pocket-books H. C. R. also kept rough accounts and made other notes which might prove interesting to economists and others. I have not yet examined them at all carefully.

and regaled her and the Aikens with the poems of Wordsworth—
which they did not invariably appreciate—or of Southey, or even
of the free-thinking, wicked Lord Byron. He was equally at
home in Unitarian and Dissenting circles, in the Anglican
atmosphere of Rydal Mount or Fox How, or with Roman
Catholic O'Connell or Quillinan. He was profoundly interested
in religious speculation, but the essentials of his own creed, as
expounded in more than one place in his *Diary* and letters, he
worked out for himself. It was, above all, a tolerant creed, as
might be expected from so tolerant a man. Nothing, for instance,
more repelled him than the conception of eternal damnation for
unbelievers, and there is a long letter on this subject to his friend
Richmond, then on the point of being ordained minister in the
Episcopalian Church of America.

Crabb Robinson's acquaintances were of every social class and
of very various capacity. Though he dearly loved a " lion,"
there was nothing of the intellectual snob about him, and he
mixed freely with all kinds of people. As a young man he loved
dancing—though he did not approve of waltzing [1] when he first
came across it at Frankfort in 1800. When he was old he often
paid anonymously the cost of an end-of-term dance for the men
of University Hall. He was a great walker, who seems to have
thought nothing of a thirty-five mile expedition, and in late
middle life he could still tire out youngsters of half his age. No
doubt connected with this physical energy were the high spirits
which distinguished him. All his friends comment upon his

---

[1] He describes it in a letter to his brother as " rolling or
turning, though the rolling is not horizontal, but perpendicular.
Yet Werter, after describing his first waltz with Charlotte, says—
and I say so too—' I felt that were I married, my wife should
waltz (or roll) with no one but myself.' Judge : The man
places the palms of his hands gently against the sides of his
partner, not far from the arm-pits. His partner does the same,
and instantly with as much velocity as possible they turn round
and at the same time gradually glide round the room."

INTRODUCTION

exuberant gaiety and light-heartedness : Mrs. Clarkson[1] says of him, when he is close on seventy, that he is " as much a boy as ever." Wordsworth, just before H. C. R. goes on his long Italian tour in 1829, calls him " a healthy creature " who talks of coming again in seven years as others would of seven days. He himself confesses : " I have through life had animal spirits in a high degree." Dr. Sadler's choice of a motto for the *Diary* is thus peculiarly appropriate :

> A Man he seems of cheerful yesterdays
> And confident to-morrows ; with a face
> Not worldly-minded, for it bears too much
> Of Nature's impress—gaiety and health,
> Freedom and hope ; but keen withal, and shrewd.
> His gestures note—and, hark! his tones of voice
> Are all vivacious as his mien and looks.
>
> *The Excursion*, Bk. VII.

This vivacity, combined with much practice in private and in public, helped him to shine in conversation as well as in more formal speaking. When he was past ninety, standing up to deliver it, he made a long and vigorous speech on the subject of the election of a professor of Logic at University College, London, speaking, he says, " with more passion than propriety," the sort of comment with which his readers become very familiar while perusing the *Diary*. But it was in private that he excelled as a talker and as a listener, and his gifts in these respects were cordially recognized by all with whom he came in contact. " The elements of conversational power in H. C. R.," says De Morgan, " were a quick and witty grasp of meaning, a wide knowledge of letters and of men-of-letters, a sufficient but not too exacting perception of the relevant, and an extraordinary power of memory." He had, too, an enormous repertory of anecdotes, and, if we may believe the rather sharp (but affectionately

---

[1] The wife of the abolitionist. She had been a kind of elder sister to him from his boyhood onwards.

INTRODUCTION

admiring) account of Bagehot, in his old age his pet stories did
duty rather too often. There is, however, no doubt of his
mastery of the art of conversation, and it was partly for this reason
that his company was so eagerly sought. As a young man and in
middle life he was constantly invited out : in his old age his
breakfast-parties were institutions. He complains that he
neglects necessary work for desultory amusement and unprofitable talk, that his days are spent to no purpose, and that he
gets through nothing of importance. But in this, as in so many
of his self-reproaches, there is little substance. Literally he added
to the gaiety of nations—by what he was, as well as by what he
said. He was, in addition, an admirable man of business, and, in
spite of his assertions to the contrary, a competent and successful
barrister with a sound practice. He was a voracious reader—of
law, history, philosophy, theology, novels, travels, and poetry—
and he wrote detailed summaries and criticisms of much that he
read. He travelled a great deal at home and abroad, and he left
no individual and no object of interest unvisited. He was never
too tired or busy to do someone a good turn, whether it were to
visit a homesick child at school, to accompany rather dull acquaintances to the exhibition, to look after the business-matters of
a widow, to collect money for someone who was in need, to
introduce the many young foreigners who were commended to
his notice, to distribute prospectuses of Coleridge's lectures, in-
vest Wordsworth's savings or lend him a carpet-bag[1] for his
travels, or conclude terms for him with a publisher or comfort him
in family afflictions.

Carlyle applied to him as a matter of course when he wanted

---

[1] My dear Friend,
       Pray meet me at Mr. Aders' on Wednesday to Breakfast.
I shall be obliged by the loan of your Carpet Bag, which you were
kind enough to offer.
                                        Ever yours,
Monday [*June* 16 ? 1828].   W. WORDSWORTH.
    12 Bryanston [St.].

INTRODUCTION

advice about the German novels he was to translate. But it was equally of course that a hundred-and-one nonentities should ask him for every variety of assistance, and that none should ever be sent away unsatisfied. He gave money, and gave it very freely and very wisely, but his generosity was shown in a thousand ways that troubled him much more than mere almsgiving.[1] Friends and acquaintances unanimously turned to him when they were in need, and their testimony in his favour is over-whelming. Like Carlyle (April 29, 1825), they knew by repeated experience his readiness to oblige, and made no scruple of apply-ing to him in any and every emergency. " I am a man," he once told Bagehot, " to whom a great number of persons entertain the very strongest objection." We can well believe that this was true, for he had his weaknesses, his crotchets, and his prejudices like other people. He could be prosy and dull and self-assertive. His society manners were not always above reproach ; for in-stance, even as a young man he frequently fell asleep in company when he did not find it amusing, or when there was music which he could not appreciate. His views on politics, too, were very pronounced, and he was unable to brook contradiction on certain matters both political and literary. Above all, he had character, personality, mind ; and such a man was unlikely, considering the number of his acquaintances and the variety of his pursuits, to pass through life without making enemies. But he had a genius for friendship, and social gifts which have outlasted him. Not only do his *Diary* and the other jottings-down of his leisure moments revivify the men whom he knew and loved. They create for him new friends in his readers, who owe to him what is almost a

---

[1] " You are the benevolent friend of all, adding to the value of every good office by the judgement which directs it."—*Flaxman to H. C. R. Feb.* 11, 1819.

" It is difficult to have less claim than myself to your services, but we have a sort of instinct that tells on whom we may venture to rely when we stand in need of a kind office."—*Miss H. M. Williams* (*minor authoress*) *to H. C. R. Mch.* 25, 1819.

INTRODUCTION

personal acquaintance with many they had otherwise vainly
wished to know in their habit as they lived. And " old Crabb "
himself moves among his comrades, still, as in a society which
has long since passed away, active, vivacious, sympathetic, understanding, and intensely alive, cheering them by his [1] " buoyant
spirit."

---

[1] Wordsworth: *Dedication to H. C. R. of the " Memorials of
an Italian Tour."* There he refers also to :

> " . . . kindnesses that never ceased to flow,
> And prompt self-sacrifice to which I owe
> Far more than any heart but mine can know."

DIARY ACCOUNT OF
BLAKE

I. 1811. July 24th . . . Late to C. Lamb's. Found a very large party there. Southey had been with Blake & admired both his designs & his poetic talents at the same time that he held him for a decided madman. Blake, he says, spoke of his visions with the diffidence that is usual with such people & did not seem to expect that he shd. be believed. He shewed S[outhey] a perfectly mad poem called *Jerusalem*. Oxford Street is in Jerusalem.

II. 1812. May 24 . . . I read W[ordsworth] some of Blake's poems ; he was pleased with some of them & considered B[lake] as having the elements of poetry a thousand times more than either Byron or Scott, but Scott he thinks superior to Campbell. I was for carrying down the descent to Rogers but W. wd. not allow it. R[ogers] has an effeminate mind, but he has not the obscure writing of C[ampbell]. . . .

III. 1815. Jan. 30. Flaxman was very chatty and pleasant. He related some curious anecdotes of Sharp the engraver, who seems the ready dupe of any and every religious fanatic & impostor who offers himself. . . . Sharp, tho' deceived by Brothers, became a warm partisan of Joanna Southcott. He endeavoured to make a convert of Blake the engraver, but as Fl. judiciously observed, such men as B[lake] are not fond of playing the 2d. fiddle. Hence B[lake] himself a seer of visions & a dreamer of dreams would not do homage to a rival claimant of the privilege of prophecy. B[lake] told F[laxman] that he had had a violent dispute with the Angels on some subject and had driven them away. . . . Excessive pride equally denoted Blake & Barry [another seer of visions].

IV. 1825. Dec. 10. Dined with Aders. A very remarkable & interesting evening. The party *Blake* the

DIARY ACCOUNT OF BLAKE

painter and Linnell,[1] also a painter & engraver to dinner
—In the Eveng. came Miss Denman & Miss Flaxman.

BLAKE

I will put down as they occur to me without method
all I can recollect of the conversation of this remarkable
man—Shall I call him Artist or Genius—or Mystic or
Madman ? Probably he is all. He has a most interesting
appearance. He is now old, pale with a Socratic countenance and an expression of great sweetness but bordering on
weakness except when his features are animated by expression & then he has an air of inspiration about him.
The conversation was on art & on poetry & on religion, but it was my object & I was successful in drawing
him out & in so getting from him an avowal of his
peculiar sentiments. I was aware before of the nature of
his impressions or I shd. at times have been at a loss to
understand him. He was shewn soon after he entered the
room some compositions of Mrs. Aders' which he cordially
praised And he brought with him an engraving of his
Canterbury pilgrims for Aders. One of the figures resembled one in one of Aders' pictures. ' They say I stole
it from this picture, but I did it 20 years before I knew of
the picture. However in my youth I was always studying
this kind of painting. No wonder there is a resemblance.'
In this he seemed to explain *humanly* what he had done,
but he at another time spoke of his paintings as being what
he had seen in his visions. And when he said *my visions*,
it was in the ordinary unemphatic tone in which we speak
of trivial matters that every one understands & cares

[1] [Reminiscences, 1825, add :] " Linnell . . . professed to
take a deep interest in Blake & his works, whether of a perfectly
disinterested character may be doubtful, as will hereafter
appear."

2

nothing about. In the same tone he said repeatedly the 'Spirit told me.' I took occasion to say—You use the same word as Socrates used. What resemblance do you suppose is there between your Spirit & the Spirit of Socrates ?[1] The same as between our countenances. He paused & added—' I was Socrates.' And then as if correcting himself, A sort of brother. I must have had conversations with him. So I had with Jesus Christ. I have an obscure recollection of having been with both of them— It was before this, that I had suggested on very obvious philosophical grounds the *impossibility* of supposing an immortal being created, an eternity a parte post, witht. an eternity a parte ante. This is an obvious truth I have been many (perhaps 30) years fully aware of. His eye brightened on my saying this And he eagerly concurred. To be sure it is impossible. We are all coexistent with God, Members of the Divine body. We are all partakers of the divine nature." In this by the bye Bl[ake] has but adopted an ancient Greek idea, Qy. of Plato. As connected with this idea I shall mention here (tho' it formed part of our talk walking homeward) that on my asking in what light he viewed the great question concerning the Divinity of Jesus Christ, He said—*He is the only God*—But then he added— ' And so am I & so are you.' Now he had just before (and that occasioned my question) been speaking of the errors of Jesus Christ. He was wrong in suffering himself to be crucified. He should not have attacked the govt. He had no business with such matters. On my enquiring how he reconciled this with the sanctity and divine qualities of Jesus, he said ' He was not then become the father '— Connecting as well as one can these fragmentary sentences it would be hard to fix Blake's station between Christianity, Platonism and Spinozism. Yet he professes to be very

[1] [Reminiscences, 1825, add :] " He smiled, & for once it seemed to me as if he had a feeling of vanity gratified."

3

hostile to Plato & reproaches Wordsworth with being not a Xn. but a Platonist.

It is one of the subtle remarks of Hume on certain religious speculations that the tendency of them is to make men indifferent to what ever takes place by destroying all ideas of good & evil. I took occasion to apply this remark to something Blake said. ' If so,' I said, ' There is no use in discipline or education, no difference betn. good & evil.' He hastily broke in on me—' There is no use in education. I hold it wrong. It is the great sin. It is eating of the tree of the Knowledge of good & evil. That was the fault of Plato—he knew of nothing but of the Virtues and Vices And good & evil. There is nothing in all that. Everything is good in God's eyes.' On my putting the obvious question, ' Is there nothing absolutely evil in what men do ' —' I am no judge of that. Perhaps not in God's Eyes.' Tho' on this & other occasions he spoke as if he denied altogether the existence of evil, And as if we had nothing to do with right and wrong—It being sufficient to consider all things as alike the work of God (I interposed with the German word of objectivity which he approved of) Yet at other times he spoke of error as being in heaven. I asked abt. the *moral* character of Dante in writing his Vision. Was he *pure* ? " *Pure* " said Blake—' Do you think there is any purity in God's eyes. The angels in heaven are no more so than we." " He chargeth his Angels with folly." He afterwards extended this to the Supreme Being. he is liable to error too. Did he not repent him that he had made Nineveh.   It is easier to repeat the personal remarks of Blake than these metaphysical speculation[s] so nearly allied to the most opposite systems. He spoke with seeming complacency of himself—Said he acted by command. The spirit said to him ' Blake, be an artist & nothing else. In this there is felicity"—His eye glistend while he spoke of devoting himself solely to

4

divine art. Art is inspiration, When Michael Angelo or Raphael or Mr. Flaxman does any of his fine things, he does them in the spirit. Bl. said ' I shd. be sorry if I had any earthly fame for whatever natural glory a man has is so much detracted from his spiritual glory. I wish to do nothing for profit. I wish to live for art. I want nothing whatever. I am quite happy.'

Among the unintelligible sentiments which he was continually expressing is his distinction between the natural & the spiritual world. The natural world must be consumed. Incidentally *Swedenborg* was spoken of. He was a divine teacher—he has done much & will do much good. He has corrected many errors of Popery & also of Luther & Calvin. Yet he also said that *Swedenborg* was wrong in endeavouring to explain to the *rational* faculty what the reason cannot comprehend. He should have left that. As B[lake] mentioned *Swedenb[org]* & *Dante* together, I wished to know whether he considered their visions of the same kind. As far as I cd. collect he does. *Dante* he said was the greater poet. He had *political* objects. Yet this, tho' wrong, does not appear in Blake's mind to affect the truth of the vision. Strangely inconsistent with this was the language of Bl[ake] about Wordsworth. W[ordsworth] he thinks is no Xn. but a Platonist—he askd me—Does he believe in the Scriptures. On my answering in the affirmative he said he had been much pained by readg. the introduction to the Excursion. It brought on a fit of illness. The passage was produced & read

> Jehovah,—with his thunder & the choir
> Of shouting angels, & the empyreal thrones—
> I *pass* them unalarmed.

This *pass them unalarmed* greatly offendd Blake. Does Mr. Wordsw[orth] think his mind can *surpass* Jehovah ? I tried to twist this passage into a sense correspondg with

5

DIARY ACCOUNT OF BLAKE

Blake's own theories but failed, And Words[worth] was finally set down as a pagan. But still with great praise as the greatest poet of the page. [Cf. Appendix, pp. 159 *et seq.*]

Jacob Boehmen was spoken of as a divinely inspired Man. Bl[ake] praised too the figures in Law's transln. as being very beautiful. Mich. Angelo cod. not have done better.—Tho' he spoke of his happiness he spoke of past sufferings & of sufferings as necessary—" There is suffering in Heaven for where there is the capacity of enjoyment, there is the capacity of pain."

I have been interrupd by a call from Talfourd in writing this account. And I can not now recollect any distinct remarks, but as Bl[ake] has invited me to go & see him I shall possibly have an opportunity again of noting what he says And I may be able hereafter to throw connection, if not system, into what I have written above. I feel great admiration & respect for him. He is certainly a most amiable man. A good creature & of his poetical & pictorial genius there is no doubt I believe in the minds of judges. Wordsworth & Lamb like his poems & the Aders his paintings.

A few other detached thoughts occur to me.

Bacon, Locke & Newton are the three great teachers of Atheism & of Satan's doctrine.

Everything is *Atheism* which assumes the reality of the Natural & Unspiritual world.

Irving He is a highly gifted man. He is a sent man, but they who are sent sometimes go further than they ought.

Dante saw Devils where I see none. I see only good. I saw nothing but good in *Calvin's* house—better than in Luther's ; he had harlots.

Swedenborg. Parts of his scheme are dangerous. His sexual religion is dangerous.

6

DIARY ACCOUNT OF BLAKE

I do not believe that the world is round. I believe it is quite flat. I objected the circumnavign—We were called to dinner at the moment & I lost the reply.[1]

The *Sun*. I have conversed with the Spiritual Sun. I saw him on Primrose-hill. He said 'Do you take me for the Greek Apollo?' 'No I said that (& Bl[ake] pointed to the sky) that is the Greek Apollo. He is Satan.[2]

" I know now what is true by internal conviction. A doctrine is told me. My heart says it must be true." I corroborated this by remarking on the impossibility of the Unlearned man judging of what are called the *external* evidences of religion, in which he heartily concurred.

I regret that I have been unable to do more than set down these seeming idle & rambling sentences. The tone & manner are incommunicable. There is a natural sweetness & gentility abt. Blake which are delightful & when he is not referring to his Visions he talks sensibly & acutely. His friend Linnel seems a great admirer. Perhaps the best thing he said was his comparison of moral with natural evil. Who shall say what God thinks evil. That is a wise tale of the Mahometans Of the Angel of the Lord that murdered the infant (alluding to the Hermit of Parnell, I suppose). Is not every infant that dies of disease in effect murdered by an angel?

[1] [Reminiscences, 1825, add :] " But objections were seldom of any use. The wildest of his assertions was made with the veriest indifference of tone as if altogether insignificant. It respected the natural and spiritual worlds. By way of example of the difference between them, he said : You never saw the Spiritual Sun. I have," etc.

[2] [Reminiscences, 1825, add :] " Not everythg. was thus absurd & there were glimpses & flashes of truth and beauty as when he cped. moral with physical evil."

7

DIARY ACCOUNT OF BLAKE

17th *Decr.* For the sake of connection I will here insert a minute of a short call I this morning made on Blake. He dwells in Fountain Court in the Strand. I found him in a small room which seems to be both a working room & a bed-room. Nothing could exceed the squalid air both of the apartment & his dress, but in spight of dirt, I might say filth, an air of natural gentility is diffused over him[,] & his wife, notwithstanding the same offensive character of her dress & appearance, has a good expression of countenance. So that I shall have a pleasure in calling on & conversing with these worthy people. But I fear I shall not make any progress in ascertaining his opinions & feelings, That there being really no system or connection in his mind, all his future conversation will be but varieties of wildness & incongruity. I found [him] at work on Dante. The book (Cary) & his sketches both before him. He shewed me his designs, of which I have nothing to say but that they evince a power of grouping & of throwing grace & interest over conceptions most monstrous & disgusting, which I shd. not have anticipated.

Our conversation began abt Dante. ' He was an Atheist, a mere politician busied abt this world as Milton was, till in his old age he returned back to God whom he had had in his childhood.'

I tried to get out from B[lake] that he meant this charge only in a higher sense And not using the word Atheism in its popular meaning. But he would not allow this. Tho' when he in like manner charged Locke with Atheism & I remarked that L[ocke] wrote on the evidences of Xnity & lived a virtuous life, he had nothg. to reply to me nor reiterated the charge of wilful deception. I admitted that Locke's doctrine leads to Atheism[1] & this seemed to satisfy him. From this subject we passed over to that of good &

---

[1] [Reminiscences, 1825, add :] " of the French school."

8

evil on which he repeated his former assertions more decidedly. He allowed indeed that there is error, mistake &c.
And if these be evil—then there is evil but these are only
negations. Nor would he admit that any education should
be attempted except that of cultivation of the imagination
& fine arts.—' What are called the vices in the natural
world are the highest sublimities in the spiritual world.'
When I asked whether if he had been a father he would
not have grieved if his child had become vicious or a great
criminal, He ansd. ' I must not regard when I am endeavouring to think rightly my own any more than other
people's weaknesses. And when I again remarked that this
doctrine put an end to all exertion or even wish to change
anything, he made no reply.—

We spoke of the Devil & I observed that when a child
I thought the Manichæan doctrine or that of two principles, a rational one. He assented to this & in confirmation asserted that he did not believe in the *omnipotence* of
God. The language of the Bible on that subject is only
poetical or allegorical. Yet soon after he denied that the
natural world is anything. It is all nothing & Satan's
empire is the empire of nothing. He reverted soon to his
favourite expression ' my visions.' I saw Milton in
Imagination And he told me to beware of being misled by his Paradise Lost. In particular he wished me to
shew the falsehood of his doctrine that the pleasures of *sex*
arose from the fall. The fall could not produce any
pleasure. I answered the fall produced a state of *evil* in
which there was a mixture of good or pleasure. And in
that sense the fall may be said to produce the pleasure.
But he replied that the fall produced only generation &
death. And then he went off upon a rambling state[-ment?]
of a Union of sexes in Man as in God, an Androgynous
state in which I could not follow him—As he spoke of
Milton's appearing to him, I asked whether he resembled
9

the prints of him.[1] He answered: 'All. Of what age did
he appear to be—Various ages. Sometimes a very old man
—he spoke of M[ilton] as being at one time a sort of
classical Atheist, And of Dante as being now with God.

Of the faculty of Vision he spoke as One he has had
from early infancy. He thinks all men partake of it, but
it is lost by not being cultivated And he eagerly assented to
a remark I made that All men have all faculties to a greater
or less degree.—I am to renew my visits & to read Wordsworth to him of Whom he seems to entertain a high idea.

17th. Made a visit to Blake of which I have written
fully in a preceding page. . . .

Saty. 24. A call on *Blake*. My 3d. Interview. I read
him Wordsworth's incomparable Ode which he heartily
enjoyed. The same half crazy crotchets abt. the two
worlds, the eternal repetition of which must in time become tiresome. Again he repeated today ' I fear Wordsworth loves Nature & Nature is the work of the Devil.
The Devil is in us, as far as we are Nature. On my enquiring whether the Devil wd. not be destroyed by God,
as being of less power, he denied that God has any power—
Asserted that the Devil is eternally created not by God
but by God's permission. And when I object[ed] that
permission implies power to prevent, he did not seem to
understand me. It was remarked that the parts of Words-

---

[1] [Reminiscences, 1825, read :] " As he spoke of frequently
seeing Milton, I ventured to ask, half ashamed at the time, wh.
of the 3 or 4 portraits in Hollis's Memoirs (Vols. in 4to) is the
most like. He answered, ' They are all like at different ages.
I have seen him as a youth & as an old man with a long flowing
beard. He came lately as an old man. He said he came to ask a
favour of me. He sd. he had committed an error in his Par.
Lost wh. he wanted me to correct in a poem or picture ; but
I declined. I said I had my own duties to perform. . . .' "

worth's Ode which he most enjoyed were the most obscure & those I the least like & comprehend.

Jan. 6, 1826. A call on Blake. I hardly feel it worth while to write down his conversation. It is so much a repetition of his former talk. He was very cordial today. I had procured him two subscriptns for his Job from Geo Procter & Basil Montagu. I paid £1 on each. This probably put him in spirits, more than he was aware of— he spoke of his being richer than ever in havg learnd to know me, & he told Mrs A[ders] he & I were nearly of an opinion. Yet I have practised no deception intentionally unless silence be so. He renewed his complaints, blended with his admiration of Wordsworth. The oddest thing he said was that he had been commandd to do certain things that is to write abt Milton And that he was applauded for refusing. He struggled with the Angels & was victor— his wife joined in the conversation.

Feb. 18 . . . Called on *Blake,* an amusing chat with him but still no novelty. The same round of extravagant & mad doctrines which I shall not now repeat but merely notice their application. He gave me, copied out by himself, Wordsworth's preface to his Excursion. At the end he has added this note. [Cf. Appendix, pp. 159 *et seq.*]

"Solomon when he married Pharaoh's daughter & became a convert to the Heathen mythology talked exactly in this way of Jehovah as a very inferior object of man's contemplations, he also passed him by unalarmed & was permitted. Jehovah dropped a tear & followed him by his spirit into the abstract void. It is called the Divine Mercy. Satan dwells in it, but mercy does not dwell in him."

Of Wordsw[orth] he talked as before. Some of his writings proceed from the Holy Ghost, but then others are the work of the Devil. However I found on this subject Blake's language more in conformity with Orthodox

Xtns. than before. He talked of the being under the direction of *Self* & *Reason* as the creature of Man & opposed to God's grace—And warmly declared that all he knew was in the Bible, but then he understands by the Bible the spiritual sense. For as to the natural sense, that Voltaire was commissioned by God to expose. I have had much intercourse with Voltaire and he said to me I blasphemed the Son of Man & it shall be forgiven me. But *they* (the enemies of V[oltaire] blasphemed the Holy Ghost in me And it shall not be forgiven them. I asked in what language Voltaire spoke. He gave an ingenious answer. ' To my sensations it was English. It was like the touch of a musical key. He touched it probably French, but to my ear it became English ! I spoke again of the *form* of the persons who appear to him. Asked why he did not *draw* them. ' It is not worth while. There are so many, the labour wd be too great. Besides there would be no Use —As to Shakesp[eare] he is exactly like the *old* Engraving, Which is called a bad one. I think it very good.

I enquired abt his writings. I have written more than Voltaire or Rousseau—6 or 7 Epic poems as long as Homer, & 20 Tragedies as long as Macbeth. He shewed me his Version (for so it may be called) of Genesis, ' As understood by a Christian Visionary." in which in a style resembling the Bible, The spirit is given. He read a passage at random. It was striking. He will not print any more. ' I write,' he says, ' when commanded by the spirits and the moment I have written I see the words fly abt the room in all directions. It is then published & the Spirits can read. My M.S.S. [are] of no further use. I have been tempted to burn my M.S.S. but my wife won't let me.' ' She is right ' said I. ' You have written these, not from yourself but by a higher order. The M.S.S. are theirs, not your property. You cannot tell what purpose they may answer unforeseen to you. He liked this & said he wd not

destroy them. His philosophy he repeated—Denying
Causation, asserting everything to be the work of God or
the Devil. That there is a constant falling off from God,
Angels becoming Devils. Every man has a Devil in him
And the conflict is eternal between a Man's self & God [1]
&c &c &c &c. He told me my copy of his Songs wd. be
five Guineas & was pleased by my manner of receiving
this information. He spoke of his horror of Money—Of
his turning pale when money had been offered him &c [2]
&c &c.

June 13. Called early on Blake. He was as *wild* as ever
with no great novelty except that he confessed a *practical*
notion which wd. do him more injury than any other I
have heard from him. He says that from the Bible he has
learned that Eine Gemeinschaft der Frauen statt finden
sollte. When I objected that Ehestand seems to be a divine
institution he referred to the Bible—'that from the beginning it was not so.' He talked as usual of the spirits,
asserted that he had committed many murders, that reason
is the only evil or sin ; & that careless gay people are better
than those who think &c &c &c.

1827. *Friday, Feb.* 2. Götzenberg[er] the young
painter from Germany called on me & I accompanied him
to Blake. We looked over Blake's Dante. Götzenberger
seemed highly gratified by the designs & Mrs Aders says
G. considers B. as the first & Flaxman as the second man
he has seen in England. The conversation was slight. I
was interpreter between them & nothing remarkable was
said by Blake. He was interested apparently by Götzenberger.

[1] [In the Reminiscences this reads :] " Every man has a devil
in himself & the conflict between his *Self* & God is perpetually
carrying on."

[2] [The Reminiscences add :] " And this was certainly un-
feigned."

13

EXTRACTS *from* LETTER
REFERRING *to* BLAKE

H.C.R. *to* DOROTHY WORDSWORTH, *Post Mark Feb.* 1826.
No. 142 *in Vol. of Letters* 1818–1826.

. . . I have above mentioned *Blake*. I forget whether I ever mentioned to you this very interesting man, with whom I am now become acquainted. Were the ' memorials ' at my hand, I should quote a fine passage in the sonnet on the Cologne Cathedral as applicable to the contemplation of this singular being. I gave your brother some poems in M.S. by him & they interested him—as well they might, for there is an affinity between them as there is between the regulated imagination of a wise poet & the incoherent dreams of a poet. Blake is an engraver by trade—a painter & a poet also whose works have been subject of derision to men in general, but he has a few admirers & some of eminence have eulogised his designs—he has lived in obscurity & poverty, to which the constant hallucinations in which he lives have doomed him. I do not mean to give you a detailed account of him. A few words will serve to inform you of what class he is. He is not so much a disciple of Jacob Böhmen & Swedenborg as a fellow visionary. He lives as they did in a world of his own. Enjoying constant intercourse with the world of spirits, He receives visits from Shakespeare, Milton, Dante, Voltaire &c &c & has given me repeatedly their very words in their conversations. His paintings are copies of what he sees in his visions. His books (& his M.S.S. are immense in quantity) are dictated from the Spirits. He told me yesterday that when he writes, it is for the spirits only.—he sees the words fly about the room the moment he has put them on paper & his book is then published. A man so favoured of course has sources of wisdom & truth peculiar to himself—I will not pretend to give you an account of his religious &

LETTER REFERRING TO BLAKE

philosophical opinions. They are a strange compound of
Christianity & Spinozaism & Platonism. I must confine
myself to what he said about your brother's works & I fear
this may lead me far enough to fatigue you in following me.
After what I have said Mr. W[ordsworth] will not be
flattered by knowing that Blake deems him the *only poet*
of the age. Nor much alarmed by hearing that like Muley
Moloch Blake thinks that he is often in his works an
Atheist. Now according to Blake Atheism consists in
worship[p]ing the natural world, which same natural
world properly speaking is nothing real, but a mere illusion
produced by Satan. Milton was for a great part of his life
an Atheist, & therefore has fatal errors in his Paradise
Lost which he has often begged Blake to confute. Dante
(tho' now with God) lived & died an Atheist. He was the
slave of the world & time   But Dante & Wordsw. in
spight of their Atheism were inspired by the Holy Ghost,
& Wordsworth's poems, (a large proportion at least) are
the work of divine inspiration. Unhappily he is left by
God to his own illusions, & then the Atheism is apparent. I had the pleasure of reading to B. in my best
style (& you know I am vain on that point & think I
read W's poems peculiarly well) the Ode on Immor-
tality. I never witnessed greater delight in any listener &
in general B. loves the poems. What appears to have disturbed his mind, on the other hand, is the preface to the
Excursion. He told me six months ago that it caused him a
bowel complaint which nearly killed him. I have in his
hand a copy of the extract [1] & the following note . . .
When I first saw B. at Mr. Aders's he very earnestly asked
me : ' Is Mr. W. a sincere real Christian ? ' In reply to
my answer he said, ' If so, what does he mean by the

[1] [For Blake's autograph copy and annotations of extracts
from Wordsworth's Preface to *The Excursion* and from Bk. 1
of *The Recluse* see Appendix, pp. 159 *et seq.*]

15

worlds to which the heaven of heavens is but a veil & who is he that shall pass Jehovah unalarmed ? "

I doubt whether what I have written will excite your & Mr W's curiosity, but there is something so delightful about the Man—tho' in great poverty he is so perfect a gentleman with such genuine dignity & independence, scorning presents & of such native delicacy in words &c &c. that I have not scrupled promising introducing him & Mr. W. together. He expressed his thanks strongly, saying, 'You do me honour. Mr W. is a great man. Besides he may convince me I am wrong about him. I have been wrong before now," &c. Coleridge has visited B. & I am told talks finely about him. That I might not encroach on a 3d. sheet I have compressed what I had to say about Blake. You must *see* him one of these days & he will interest you at all events, whatever character you give to his mind . .

EXTRACTS *from the* REMINI-SCENCES *of* BLAKE
(a) 1810

I WAS amusing myself this Spring by writing an account of the insane poet & painter engraver, *Blake*   Perthes of Hamburg had written to me asking me to send him an article for a new German Magazine entitled *Vaterländische Annalen* wh. he was abt to set up. And Dr. Malkin having in the memoirs of his son given an acct of this extraordinary genius with Specimens of his poems, I resolved out of these to compile a paper. And this I did, & the paper was translated by Dr. Julius, who many years afterwards introduced himself to me as my translator. It appears in the single number of the 2d. vol. of the *Vaterländische Annalen.* For it was at this time that Buonaparte united Hamburg to the French Empire, on wh. Perthes manfully gave up the Magazine, saying, as he had no longer a Vaterland, there cd. be no *Vaterländische Annalen.* But before I drew up this paper, I went to see a Gallery of Blake's paintings, wh. were exhibited by his brother, a hosier in Carnaby Market ; the entrance was 2/6, catalogue included.[1] I was deeply interested by the Catalogue as well as by the pictures. I took 4, telling the brother I hoped he wd. let me come in again. He said, ' Oh! as often as you please.' I dare say such a thing had never happened before or did afterwards.[2]

I afterwards became acquainted with Blake & will postpone till hereafter what I have to relate of this extraordinary character, whose life has since been written very inadequately by Allan Cunningham in his Lives of the English artists. . .

[1] [Reminiscences, 1825, read :] " This catalogue I possess, and it is a very curious exposure of the state of the artist's mind. I wished to send it to Germany and to give a copy to Lamb and others, so I took four. . . ."

[2] [*See* page 20 for Lamb's opinion of this catalogue.]

REMINISCENCES OF BLAKE

(b) 1825–1827

IT was at the latter end of the year 1825 that I put in writing my recollections of this remarkable man. The larger portion are under the date of the 10th of Decr.[1] He died in the year 1827. I have therefore now revised what I wrote on the 10th of Decr. & afterwards, & without any attempt to reduce to order or make consistent the wild & strange, strange rhapsodies uttered by this insane man of genius, thinking it better to put down what I find as it occurs, tho' I am aware of the objection that may justly be made to the recording the ravings of insanity in which it may be said there can be found no principle, as there is no ascertainable law of mental association wh. is obeyed ; & from wh. therefore nothing can be learned.

This would be perfectly true of *mere* madness, but does not apply to that form of insanity or lunacy called Monomania, & may be disregarded in a case like the present in which the subject of the remark was unquestionably what a German wd. call a " *Verunglückter Genie* " whose theosophic dreams bear a close resemblance to those of *Swedenborg* ; whose genius as an artist was praised by no less men than *Flaxman* & *Fuseli*, & whose poems were thought worthy republication by the biographer of *Swedenborg*, *Wilkinson*, & of which Wordsworth said, after reading a number. " They were the " Songs of Innocence & Experience," showing the two opposite states of the human soul." There is no doubt this poor man was mad, but there is something in the madness of this man which interests me more than the sanity of Lord Byron or Walter Scott !—

The German painter Götzenberger, (a man indeed who ought not to be named *after the others* as an authority for my writing abt Blake) said on his returning to Germany

[1] [See *ante*, pp. 1–7.]

18

REMINISCENCES OF BLAKE

about the time at which I am now arrived, " I saw in England many men of talents, but only 3 men of Genius, Coleridge, Flaxman & Blake, & of these Blake was the greatest." I do not mean to intimate my assent to this opinion, nor to do more than supply such materials as my intercourse with him furnishes to an uncritical narrative, to wh. I shall confine myself. I have written a few sentences in these reminiscences already, those of the year 1810. I had not then begun the regular Journal which I afterwards kept. I will therefore go over the ground again & introduce these recollections of 1825 by a reference to the slight knowledge I had of him before, & what occasioned my taking an interest in him, not caring to repeat what Cunningham has recorded of him in the volume of his Lives of the British Painters, &c. &c. except thus much. It appears that he was born [on 28th November 1757]. *Dr. Malkin* our Bury Grammar School Head Master published in the year 1806 a memoir of a very precocious child who died [blank in MS.] years old, & he prefixed to the Memoir an engraving of a portrait of him by Blake, & in the vol. he gave an acct. of Blake as a painter & poet & printed some specimens of his poems, viz. *The Tiger* & ballads & mystical lyrical poems, all of a wild character, & M[alkin] gave an account of visions wh. Blake related to his acquaintance. I knew that Flaxman thought highly of him, & tho' he did not venture to extol him as a genuine Seer, yet he did not join in the ordinary derision of him as a madman. Without having seen him, yet I had already conceived a high opinion of him, & thought he wd. furnish matter for a paper interesting to Germans. And therefore when *Fred. Perthes* the patriotic publisher at Hamburg wrote to me in 1810, requesting me to give him an article for his Patriotische Annalen, I thought I cd. do no better than send him a paper on Blake [1] . . .

[1] [*See* Extract (*a*), p. 17.]

REMINISCENCES OF BLAKE

Lamb was delighted with the Catalogue, especially with the description of a painting afterwards engraved, & connected with wh. is an anecdote that unexplained wd. reflect discredit on a most amiable & excellent man, but wh. Flaxman considered to have been the wilful act of *Stod-[d]art*. It was after the friends of Blake had circulated a subscription paper for an engraving of his *Canterbury Pilgrims* that *Stod[d]art* was made a party to an engraving of a painting of the same subject by himself. Stoddart's work is well-known : Blake's is known by very few. Lamb preferred it greatly to Stoddart's & declared that Blake's description was the finest criticism he had ever read of Chaucer's poem.

In this Catalogue, Blake writes of himself in the most outrageous language, says " This artist defies all competition in colouring," that none can beat him, for none can beat the Holy Ghost ; that he & Raphael & Michael Angelo were under the divine influence, while Corregio & Titian worshipped a lascivious & therefore cruel devil, Rubens a proud devil &c. He declared, speaking of colour, Titian's men to be of leather & his women of chalk, & ascribed his own perfection in colouring to the advantage he enjoyed in seeing daily the primitive men walking in their native nakedness in the mountains of Wales.—There were about 30 oil paintings, the colouring excessively dark & high, the veins black & the colour of the primitive men very like that of the red Indians. In his estimation they wd. probably be the primitive men. Many of his designs were unconscious imitations. This appears also in his published works,—the designs to *Blair's Grave*, wh. Fuseli & Schiavonetti highly extolled, & in his designs to illustrate *Job* published after his death for the benefit of his widow. 23.2.52.

To this Catalogue & to the printed poems, the small pamphlet wh. appeared in 1783, the edition put forth by

REMINISCENCES OF BLAKE

Wilkinson, 'The Songs of Innocence,' other works &c already mentioned, to wh. I have to add the first two books of Young's Night Thoughts, & Allan Cumberland's Life of him, I now refer, & will confine myself to the memorandums I took of his conversation. I . . . for the first time dined in his company at the Aders'. . . .[1] He was then 68 years of age. He had a broad, pale face, a large full eye with a benignant expression ; at the same time a look of languor except when excited, & then he had an air of inspiration, but not such as without a previous acquaintance with him, or attending to *what* he said, would suggest the notion that he was insane. There was nothing *wild* about his look & though very ready to be drawn out to the assertion of his favourite ideas, yet with no warmth as if he wanted to make proselytes. Indeed one of the peculiar features of his scheme as far as it was consistent was indifference & a very extraordinary degree of tolerance & satisfaction with what had taken place, a sort of pious & humble optimism, not the scornful optimism of *Candide*. But at the same time that he was very ready to praise he seemed incapable of envy, as he was of discontent. He warmly praised some composition of Mrs Aders[2]. . . .

25.2.52.

On the 17th I called on him in his house in Fountains Court in the Strand. The interview was a short one, & what I saw was more remarkable than what I heard. He was at work engraving in a small bedroom, light & looking out on a mean yard—everythg. in the room squalid, & indicating poverty except himself. And there was a natural gentility about, & an insensibility to the seeming poverty which quite removed the impression. Besides, his linen was clean, his hand white & his air quite unembarrassed when he begged me to sit down, as if he were in a palace. There was but one chair in the room

---

[1] [See *ante*, pp. 1–2.]   [2] [See *ante*, pp. 2–7.]

besides that on wh. he sat. On my putting my hand to it, I found that it would have fallen to pieces if I had lifted it. So, as if I had been a Sybarite, I said with a smile, ' Will you let me indulge myself ? ' And I sat on the bed and near him. And during my short stay there was nothing in him that betrayed that he was aware of what to other persons might have been even offensive, not in his person, but in all about him.

His wife I saw at this time, & she seemed to be the very woman to make him happy. She had been formed by him. Indeed otherwise she cd. not have lived with him. Notwithstanding her dress, wh. was poor & dirty, she had a good expression in her countenance—& with a dark eye, had remains of beauty in her youth. She had that virtue of virtues in a wife, an implicit reverence of her husband. It is quite certain that she believed in all his visions, & on one occasion, not this day, speaking of his visions she said, ' You know dear, the first time you saw God was when you were 4 years old. And he put his head to the window & set you ascreaming.' In a word, she was formed on the Miltonic model, & like the first wife, Eve, worshipped God in her husband, he being to her what God was to him. Vide Milton's Par. Lost, passim.

26.2.52.

He was making designs or engraving, I forget which— Cary's Dante was before [him]. He shewed me some of his designs from Dante of which I do not presume to speak. They were too much above me. But Götzenberger, whom I afterwds. took to see them expressed the highest admiration of them. They are in the hands of *Linnell*, the painter, & it has been suggested, are reserved by him for publication when Blake may have become an object of interest to a greater number than he can be at this age [1] . . .

27.2.52.

[1] [See *ante*, pp. 8—9.]

22

REMINISCENCES OF BLAKE

1826. On the 24th I called a second time on him, &
on this occasion it was that I read to him *Wordsworth's
Ode* on the supposed pre-existent state, & the subject of
W.'s religious character was discussed when we met on the
18th of Feb. & the 12th of May. I will here bring together
W. Blake's declaratns. concerning W. & set down his
marginalia in the 8vo. edit. A.D. 1815. Vol. 1. I had been
in the habit when reading this marvellous Ode to friends,
to omit one or two passages, especially that beginning

> But there's a tree, of many one

lest I shd. be rendered ridiculous, being unable to explain
precisely *what* I admired—not that I acknowledged this
to be a fair test. But with Blake I cd. fear nothing of the
kind, & it was this very Stanza wh. threw him almost into
an hysterical rapture. His delight in W.'s poetry was in-
tense. Nor did it seem less notwithstanding by the reproaches he continually cast on W. for his imputed worship of nature, wh. in the mind of Blake constituted
Atheism.   28.2.52.

The combn. of the warmest praise with imputations
which from another wd. assume the most serious character
& the liberty he took to interpret as he pleased, rendered it
as difficult to be offended as to reason with him. The eloquent descriptions of Nature in W.'s poems were con-
clusive proof of atheism, for whoever believes in Nature
said B. disbelieves in God. For Nature is the work of the
Devil. On my obtaining from him the declaration that the
Bible was the work of God, I referred to the commencement
of Genesis " In the beginning God created the Heaven &
the Earth." But I gained nothing by this, for I was triumph-
antly told that this God was not Jehovah, but the Elohim,
& the doctrine of the Gnostics repeated with sufficient
consistency to silence one so unlearned as myself.[1] . .

[1] [See *ante*, pp. 15–16.]

23

REMINISCENCES OF BLAKE

I lent him the 8vo. ed. of 2 vols. of W.'s poems wh. he had in his possession at the time of his death. They were sent me then. I did not recognise the pencil notes he made in them to be his for some time, & was on the point of rubbing them out, under that impression when I made the discovery. The following are found in the 5th Vol.:—
In the fly-leaf under the words Poems referring to the Period of Childhood.   29.2.52.
" I see in Wordsw. the natural man rising up agst. the spiritual man continually & then he is no poet, but a heathen philosopher at Enmity agst. all true poetry or inspiration." Under the first poem

> 3 " And I cd. wish my days to be
>   Bound each to each by natural piety "

he had written " There is no such thing as natural piety because the natural man is at enmity with God." p. 43 under the verses to H. C. six years old. " This is all in the highest degree imaginative & equal to any poet, but not superior. I cannot think that real poets have any competition. None are greatest in the Kingdom of God. It is so in Poetry." page 44 " On the influence of natural objects." at the bottom of the page : " Natural objects always did & now do weaken, deaden & obliterate Imagination in me. W. must know that what he writes valuable is not to be found in Nature. Read Michael Angelo's Sonnet, Vol. 2, p. 179."—that is the one beginning

> " No mortal object did these eyes behold
>   When first they met the placid light of thine."

It is remarkable that Blake whose judgements were in most points so very singular, on one subject closely connected with W.'s poetical reputation should have taken a very commonplace view. Over the heading of the " Essay supplementary to the Preface " at the end of the vol. he wrote " I do not know who wrote these Prefaces : they are very mischievous & direct contrary to W.'s own practice " (p. 341). This is not the defence of his own style in opposition to what is called Poetic Diction, but a sort of historic vindication of the *unpopular* poets. On Macpherson, p. 364. W. wrote with the severity with wh. all great writers have written of him. Blake's comment below was :—" I believe both Macpherson & Chatterton, that what they say is ancient is so." & in the following page : " I own myself an admirer of Ossian equally with any other poet whatever, Rowley & Chatterton also." And at the end of this Essay he wrote " It appears to me as if the last paragraph beginning " Is it the result of the whole " & it [?] was written by another hand & mind from the rest of these Prefaces : they are the opinions of [blank in MS.] landscape painter. Imagination is the divine vision not of the World, nor of Man, nor from Man as he is a natural man, but only as he is a spiritual Man. Imagination has nothing to do with Memory."   1.3.52.

⋅ ⋅ ⋅ ⋅ ⋅ ⋅

   In the No : of the Gents. Magazine for last Jan. [1852] there is a letter by *Cromek* to Blake, printed in order to convict B[lake] of selfishness. It cannot possibly be substantially true. I may elsewhere notice it.

⋅ ⋅ ⋅ ⋅ ⋅ ⋅ ⋅ ⋅

   It was, I believe on the 7th of December that I saw him last. I had just heard of the death of Flaxman, a man whom he professed to admire, & was curious how he wd. receive the intelligence. It was as I expected. He had been ill during the summer, & he said with a smile, ' I thought I shd. have gone first.' He then said, ' I cannot think of death as more than the going out of one room into another.' And Flaxman was no longer thought of. He relapsed into his ordinary train of thinking. Indeed I had by this time learned that there was nothing to be gained by frequent intercourse, & therefore it was that after this interview I was not anxious to be frequent in my visits. This day he said, ' Men are born with an Angel & a Devil.' This he himself interpreted as Soul & Body. And as I have long since said of the strange sayings of a man who enjoys a high reputation " It is more in the language than the thoughts that the singularity is to be looked for." And this day he spoke of the Old Testament as if it were the Evil Element. " Christ, he said, took much after his Mother & in so far he was one of the worst of men." On my asking him for an instance, he referred to his turning the money changers out of the temple—he had no right to do that. He digressed into a condemnation of those who sit in judgment on others. " I have never known a very bad man who had not somethg. very good abt him." Speaking of the Atonement in the ordinary Calvinistic sense, he said " It is a horrible doctrine ; if another pay your debt, I do not forgive it." I have no account of any other call, but this is probably an omission. I took Götzenberger to see him & he met the Masqueriers in my Chambers. Masquerier was not the man to meet him. He could not humour B. nor understand the peculiar sense in wh. B. was to be recd.

1827. My journal of this year contains nothing abt Blake.[1] But in Jan. 1828 Barron Field & myself called on Mrs. Blake. The poor old lady was more affected than I expected she would be at the sight of me. She spoke of her husband as dying like an Angel. She informed us that she was going to live with Linnell as his housekeeper, & we understood that she would live with him. And he, as it were, to farm her services & take all she had. The Engravings of Job were his already. Chaucer's Canterbury Pilgrims were hers. I took 2 copies ; one I gave to C. Lamb. Barron Field took a proof.

[1] [But see *ante*, p. 13, under Feb. 2, 1827.]

REMINISCENCES OF BLAKE

Mrs. Blake died within a few years. And since Blake's death Linnell has not found the market. I took for granted he would seek for Blake's works. Wilkinson printed a small edition of his poems including the " Songs of Innocence & Experience " a few years ago. And Monkton Milne talks of printing an edition. I have a few coloured engravings, but B[lake] is still an object of interest exclusively to men of imaginative taste & psychological curiosity. I doubt much whether these Memoirs will be of any use to this small class.   1.3.52.

I have been reading since the life of Blake by Allan Cunningham Vol. 11, p. 143 of his Lives of the Painters. It recognises perhaps more of Blake's merit than might have been expected of a Scotch realist.   22.3.52.

REMINISCENCES: COLERIDGE, WORDSWORTH, LAMB, &c.[1]

I HAVE a distinct recollection of reading the Monthly Review of the 1st. vol. of Coleridge's poems before I went abroad in 1800 & of the delight the extracts gave me, & my friend Mrs. Clarkson having become intimate with him, he [became] an object of interest with me from my return from Germany in 1805. And when he deliverd lectures in the year 1808, Mrs Clarkson engaged me to interest myself in his lectures I needed no persuasion. I did hear some of his lectures that year but I had then engagements wh. put it out of my power to attend them regularly, but I wrote to her two letters in that year wh. she preserved & wh. have been printed by Mrs. Henry Coleridge in her vol. of Notes & Lectures on Shakespear. Pickering. 1849. They give me no pleasure in the perusal, but there was such a want of materials for the account Mrs. C[oleridge] wished to give of her father's lectures that she thought it worth while to print even these. But at the time of my attending these lectures I had no personal acquaintance with C. I have a letter from him written in May 1808, sending me an order to hear his lectures in wh. he says : " Nothing but endless interruptions & the necessity of dining out far oftener than is either good for me or pleasant to me, joined with the reluctance to move (partly from exhaustion by company I cannot keep out, for one cannot dare not be always 'not at home ' or ' very particularly engaged,' & the last very often will not serve my turn) these added to my bread & cheese employments + my lectures which are—bread & cheese, i.e. a very losing bargain in a pecuniary view, have prevented me day after day from returning your kind calls. Piu vorrei piu non posso. In the mean time I have left your name with the old woman & the attendants in the office as one to whom I am always at home when I am at home. For Wordsworth has taught me to desire your acquaintance & to esteem you . . . & need I add that anyone so much regarded by Mrs. C[larkson], (whom I love even as my very own sister, whose Love for me, with Wordsworth's sister, wife & wife's sister form almost the only happiness I have on earth) can ever be indifferent to . . . &c. &c. &c. S. T. C.

Yet I find among my papers two 8vo. pages being minutes of C.'s lecture, Feb. 5, 1808 wh. I may not here refer to because they contain nothing personal.

It was not till 1811 that I kept anything like a diary. I am about to make extracts from it & I will extract from it & from the few letters I find from or concerning C. what I think worth preserving, & so set it apart among my Reminiscences. (9,7,49)

It has since occurred to me that it will be more convenient if I combine in one continuous article all my reminiscences of Coleridge, Wordsworth, & Lamb. They all belong to one class & comprehend notices of Men of Genius, who tho' of a very different kind, were friends to each other, and besides, I became acquainted with them through the same friend Mrs. Clarkson. I may perhaps, not as their equal by any means, also insert what I have to say of their very excellent friend & an admirable writer, Southey, & also their enemy Hazlitt—in short all of this set or clique as they for some time were considered.

I begin these minutes after I had written the year 1810 & all the preceding, at which time my acquaintance with all of them had commenced & I have already written about them, but my former reminiscences are not in my possession. I therefore begin with the year 1811, & shall take chronologically what I find in my Diary.

COLERIDGE, WORDSWORTH, LAMB, &c.

Jan. 8. I soon found that tho' C. Lamb was a warm lover of Wordsw.'s poetry yet that he thought Coleridge the greater man. He preferred *The Ancient Mariner* to anything W. had written. Among W.'s poems, L. praised *Hart Leap Well*, not *The Leech-Gatherer*— also the *Sonnets*. He urged agst. Wordsw. what lies essentially in his *subjective* poetry, that W. cannot, like Shakesp[eare], become everything he pleases.

I had written thus far when I found a few pages written in Novr. & December 1810 devoted entirely to Coleridge. I will transfer the substance of them to this paper.

14th Nov. Saw Coleridge for the first time in private at Charles Lamb's. A short interview which allowed of little opportunity for the display of his peculiar powers. He related to us that Jeffrey, the Editor of *The Edinb. Review* had lately called on him & assured him that he was a great admirer of Wordsworth's poetry, that his *Lyrical Ballads* were always on his table &c; That he, (W.) had been attacked in the Rev[iew] only because the Errors of Men of Genius ought to be exposed. Jeffrey, he [C.] added was towards me even flattering : he was like a schoolboy who, having tried his man & been thrashed, becomes contentedly a fag. (10.7.49)

Jeffrey spoke of Campbell to Coleridge, who had also been visited by him & whom C[oleridge] called 'a chicken-breasted fellow.' Camp., said J. is my intimate friend, but he is sadly envious. You outshone him in conversation & I am sure he therefore hates you thoroughly.'

15th Nov. at Lamb's. Coler., his friend Morgan, M. Burney &c. &c. C. spoke with warm praise of Wordsw: but blamed him for attaching himself to the low in his desire to avoid the artificial in genteel life. He should have recollected that verse being the language of

30

passion required a style raised in harmony with it. One asks why tales so simple were not in prose. He 'with malice prepense' cast his reflexion on objects that do not naturally excite it. In the *Gypsies* for instance, had the whole world stood idle, more powerful considerations need not have been brought to expose the evil, than are brought forward on their account.

Of *Kant* he spoke in high praise. In his " Himmel-system " he combined the genius of Newton & Burnet. He praised the *Träume eines Geistersehers*, would translate his *Sublime & Beautiful* & thought the *Kritik der Urtheils-kraft* the most astonishing of his works.

Fichte & Schelling he said will be found at last wrong where they have left their master, towards whom they shewd ingratitude. *Fichte* a great logician, Schelling perhaps a greater man. Schelling's *System* resolves itself into fanaticism not better than that of Jakob Böhmen.

C. had known *Tieck* at Rome but was not aware of his eminence as a poet. He conceded to *Goethe* universal talent, but felt his want of *moral life*, the defect of his poetry. *Schiller* he spoke more kindly of. He quoted " Nimmer, dass glaubt mir, erscheinen die Götter " (N.B. He has translated it). He censured the Graeco-manie of S.'s last dramas.

Jean Paul. He said that J. P's wit consisted not in pointing out analogies in themselves striking, but in finding unexpected analogies. You admire, not the things com-bined, but the act of combination. And he applied this to *Windham*. N.B. It did not occur to me then to remark as it does now, that this is the character of *all* wit, & that that wh. he contrasted with it as a different kind of wit, is not wit, but acuteness.

He made an elaborate distinction between Fancy & Imagination. The excess of fancy is delirium, of imagn., mania. Fancy is the arbitrary bringing together of things

31

that lie remote & forming them into a Unity : the materials lie ready for the fancy which acts by a sort of juxtaposition. On the other hand the Imagination under some excitement generates & produces a form of its own. The ' Seas of Milk & Ships of Amber ' (? Belvidera) he quoted as fanciful delirium. As a sort of disease of imagination he related what occurred to himself. He had been watching intensely the motions of a kite among the mountains of Westmoreland, when he, on a sudden, saw two kites in an opposite direction. This illusion lasted some time. At last he discovered that the two kites were the fluttering branches of a tree beyond a wall.

18th Nov. At Godwin's. Northcote, the Dawes etc. Coleridge made himself very merry at the expense of *Fuseli*, whom he always called *Fuzzle* or *Fuzly*. He told a story of Fuseli's being on a visit at Liverpool at a time when unfortunately he had to divide the attention of the public with a Prussian soldier who had excited great notice by his enormous powers of eating, & the annoyance was aggravated by persons persisting to consider the soldier as his countryman. He spent his last evening at Dr. Crompton's, when *Roscoe* (whose visitor F. was) took an opportunity to give a hint to the party that no one shd. mention the glutton. The admonition unfortunately was not heard by a lady who, turning to the great Academician & lecturer, said, ' Well Sir, your countryman has been surpassing himself.' ' Madam,' growled the irritated artist, ' the fellow is no countryman of mine.' ' Why, he is a foreigner. Have you not heard what he has been doing ? He has eaten a live cat.' ' A live cat,' everyone repeated, except Fuseli whose rage was roused by the exclamation of Mrs. Currie, a lady famous for her blunders. ' Dear me ! Mr. Fuseli, that is a fine subject for your pencil.' ' *My* pencil, Madam ?.' ' To be sure, Sir. The *horrible* is your *forte*, you know.' ' You mean the *terrible*, Madam,'

32

he replied with an assumed composure, at the same time muttering between his teeth, ' if a silly woman could mean anything.'

December 20*th*. Met Coleridge by accident with Cha. & Mary Lamb. As I entered, he was apparently arguing in favour of Christianity. At the same time contending that Miracles were not an essential in the Christian System, he insisted that they were not brought forward as proofs ; that miracles were acknowledged as having been performed by others as well as the true believers. Pharaoe's magicians wrought miracles also, tho' those of Moses were more powerful. In the New Testamt. the appeal is made to the knowl. which the believer has of the truths of his religion, not to the wonders wrought to make him believe.

Of *Jesus Christ* he asserted that he was a Platonic philosopher, & when Christ spoke of his identity with the Father, he spoke in a Spinosistic or Pantheistic sense, accordg to which he could truly say that his transcendental sense was *one* with God, while his empirical sense retained its finite nature.

I related the argument of Wieland's Agathodæmon (who represents J[esus] C[hrist]—like the Pythagorean *Apollonius*, a philanthropic impostor). C. dissented from this representation. He was convinced that J. C. felt the truth of all he affirmed & knew that he was inspired. But on my remarking that, in a certain sense, everyone who utters a truth may be said to be inspired, C. assented to this & afterwards named *Fox* & other of the Quakers, Mad. *Guyon*, St. *Theresa* &c. as being *also* inspired.

On my suggesting in the form of a question, That an eternal & absolute truth, like those of religion, could not be *proved* by an accidental fact of history, he at once assented, & declared it to be inadvisable to ground the belief of Christianity on historic evidence : He went so far as to affirm that religious belief is an act not of the understanding

33   c

but of the will. To become a believer, one must love the doctrine & must resolve with passion to believe, Not sit down coolly to enquire whether he shd. believe or no. Notwithstanding the sceptical tendency of such opinions, he added that accepting as he did Christianity in its spirit in conformity with his own philosophy, he was content for the sake of its divine truths to receive as articles of faith, the miracles of the New Testament, taken in their literal sense. *N.B.* It occurs to me now that I perhaps ought to have written instead of *receive as articles of faith, leave undisputed.* I am reminded in writing this of one of the famous Pensées of Pascal which Jacobi quotes repeatedly. I cite from memory. " It is this which distinguishes spiritual from material truths. You must believe the first before you can understand them. You must understand the last before you can believe them.

Coleridge added to this warm praise of Spinoza, Jacobi on Spinoza, Schiller *Über die Sendung Moses* etc., & he assented to a remark of mine that the error of Spinoza seems to be the attempting to reduce to demonstration what was matter of faith.

A talk abt. Shakespear[e]. C. Lamb spoke with admiration of *Love's Labour[s] Lost, Mids[ummer] Night's Dream.* Coler[idge] did not concur. But they agreed in this, that not a line of *Titus Andronicus* could have been written by Shakesp[eare], wh.[1] Lamb ascribed to Marlowe from its resemblance to *The Jew of Malta.*[1]

Dec. 23d. Coleridge at Collier's. Coleridge exhibited his inconsistency by beginning with praising the K[ing] Geo[rge] III, to whose firmness he said we were indebted for our not yielding to the French. Yet being pressed, he admitted that the King was an enemy to the Americans, & a friend to the Slave Trade, & also that another system of government might have saved the country from infinite

[1 This is scratched out in H. C. R.'s MS.]

34

misery. So that the poor old K[ing] had at last nothing left him but his personal morals & their influence on the upper classes.

This day his chief talk was on Shakesp[eare]. The leading ideas are those that have been published recently by Mrs. Coler[idge] & my notes are of less value. I shall therefore abridge them. The one thought which he this eveng. expressed in different ways was, that Shakesp. meant in his *Iago* & in his *Rich[ard] III* to exhibit the pride of intellect & the same in *Falstaff*, but at the same time to show the superiority of moral sense over mere intellect. (See the Lectures. Vol. 1, pp. 187, 257.) *Falstaff* had more intellect than the *Prince* & did not think it was possible for the Prince to escape from his influence, but the higher moral charr. of the Prince raises him above his insidious companion. Of *R.* 3 he wrote but little. He found it a stock play & wrote merely what expressed R's character—certainly not the scene with Qu. Anne. In *Pericles* we see how Sh. handled a piece he had to refit for representation. He began with indifference, only now & then putting in a word, but interesting himself in his subj[ec]t, the last two acts are almost altogether by him.

Hamlet he considered in a point of view which seems to agree very well with that taken in *Wilhelm Meister*. H[amlet] said C., is one whose internal images (*ideal*) are so vivid, that all actual objects are faint & dead to him ; hence his soliloquies on the nature of man, his disregard of life & hence his vacillations & convulsive energies. I re-marked that it seemed to me unaccountable why Sh. did not make Hamlet destroy himself. C. said that S. meant to show that even such a character was forced to be the slave of chance—a salutary moral lesson. He remained to the last inept & immovable ; not even the spirit of his father could rouse him to action.

Milton. He spoke of Milton as decidedly an aristocrat &

35

an enemy to popular elections. His works have only one exceptional passage—his vindication of Cromwell's purging the House of Commons. The execution of *Par[adise] Regained* is superior to that of *Par[adise] Lost*, & that is all Milton meant in giving it a preference to the *Par[adise] Lost*. C. took occasion to assert his approbn. of the death of Charles.

Hartley. Of Hartley's doctrine of assocn. This is as old as Aristotle. Hartley understood it better when he reached the 2d. vol. of his great work & would not rest the evidce of Christy. on it. '*Thought*,' said C., 'is a breaking thro the law of Association. They who wd. build everything on association are too apt to leave out of account the things associated.

Taylor's *Holy Living & Holy Dying* he declared to be a perfect poem in its details. Its rhythm may be compared with the *Night Thoughts*.

As usual he spoke with contempt of *Locke's Essay*. It led to the destruction of metaphysical science by encouraging the unlearned to think that with good sense they might dispense with study. The popularity of *Locke's Essay* he ascribed to his political position : he was the advocate of the new dynasty agst the old & as a religious writer, agst the Infidel, tho' he was but an Arian. And the *national* vanity was gratified. He & Newton were pitted agst Leibnitz. It was to lessen Leibnitz that Voltaire set up Locke. He assented to my remark that Atheism might be demonstrated out of Locke. He praised Stillingfleet as the opponent of Locke's *Essay*. 11.7.49.

1811. I now resume from my journal.

Jan. 23d. I met *Coleridge* with Rickman, Morgan &c. at C. Lamb's. The conversation was on politics & on no subject did I like him so little. He was very vehement agst. granting to the Irish even equal civil rights because then they would claim equal power. The Cath[olic] spirit, said C., is incorrigible. The priests wd. claim the tithes & require to have their religion established. " I would not give equal power to 3 millions of barbarians.' I replied ' I wd. give them equal rights because they could not convert their rights into power without ceasing to be barbarians.' C. said he wd. hang every Irishman who refused to be considered as an Englishman. I denied that a Union forced on the nation agst their will could have a magical influence on them. I tried to draw a parallel bet. the relation of the Italians to the French, & that of the Irish to the English, wh. C. denied to be valid. The Italians, he said, are not inferior to the French as the Irish are to the English. The original conquest of Irel[and], he said, by England, was for their benefit. They wd. otherwise have been a nest of pirates.

Coler. & Rickman both justified the expense of our civil jurisprudence. Lawyers, said C., are now what the clergy race were, the depositories of intellect. It is no evil that they shd. form a rich, powerful & honoured body. Cheap law makes lawyers base & the whole nation litigious. This, he sd., was seen in Sicily.

29th Jan. With Coler. at Rickman's. He talked on the Drama & Shakesp. He contrasted, as he did afterwards in his lectures, the Greek with the Shakesp. drama : Shakesp. fools supplied the place of the Greek chorus ; both represented a passionless spectator.

Coleridge & Rickman both abused the Reformers, but Coler. notwithst[andin]g expressed his contempt for Pitt. The alarm of 1793 was a panic of property which misled the Engl. government into a series of blunders wh. laid the foundation of French dominion.

He justified the Usury Laws agt. Bentham. By generating a contempt for usurers, many were deterred from becoming mere money-lenders. Genoa fell because their merchants were changed into usurers. ' In money loans one party is in sorrow. In the traffic of merchandise, both

37

parties gain & rejoice. Of criminal law he said that its
object is not merely to prevent mischievous acts : it is to
be a moral instructor.

13th March. With Coler. who called on me. He spoke
abt. a translation I had made of a German tale & I shd.
have been flattered had he spoken in the same way of the
writing of a stranger, but Coler. like all kind-hearted men,
has a pleasure in giving pleasure.

Speaking of Southey today, he said S. was not competent
to appreciate Spanish poetry ; he wanted modifying
power. He was a jewel setter ; whatever he found to his
taste he formed it into, or made it the ornament of a story.

March 24. A call on Coler. He expatiated largely
on the powerful effect of brotherly & sisterly love
in the formn. of char[acte]r. Certain peculiarities in his
wife, Mrs. Southey, Mrs. Lovell he ascribed to their
having no brother. I recollect too, but it was on some other
occasion, his saying that he envied Wordsworth his having
had a sister & that his own character had suffered from the
want of a sister. To-day he also spoke of *incest*. The
universal horror he ascribed not to *instinct* (if I mistake not
Southey, he said, believed in the *instinct*). He was of opinion
that fatal consequences had been found to follow from the
intercourse. And therefore a religious horror had been
industriously excited by priests—he spoke of novelty as
exciting, & of habitual presence as repressing desire.

March 29. With Coler. at Hazlitt's. Before Lamb
came, Coler. praised his *serious* conversation & Hazlitt
ascribed his puns to *humility*.

C. in his abuse of the Scotch, said, Edinb[urgh] is a
talking town & the Edinb. Rev. is a concentration of all
the smartness of all Scotland. When, in an Edinb. Conver-
sazione, a spark is elicited, it is instantly caught, preserved, &
brought to the Rev[iew]. He denied humour to the nation.

Of *Rogers* he said that he was the slave of public opinion.

38

He at first eulogised Bloomfield, but when the world neglected him, he neglected him too.

Abstraction was spoken of. Hazlitt sd. he had learned from painting how hard it is to have an idea of an individual object. At first we have only a general idea, that is, vague, broken, imperfect. On my saying that this is all generally meant by *general* idea, Hazlitt said he had no other. Coler. said, ' We cannot bring an individual object under a class with[ou]t having a previous notion of the class." This, by the bye, is Kantian logic, tho in my journal I perceive I was not aware of this.

Mar. 30. With Coler. & Hazlitt at Lamb's. Coler. spoke with a kindness of Godwin wh. gratified me. G., it was said, was wounded by Southey's Rev[iew] of his *Life of Chaucer* in the *Annual Review*. S.'s severity he ascribed to the habit of reviewing. He did not justify the rev[iew] but said its severity proceeded from the great purity of S.'s own mind. Such men are *blunt* in their moral feelings,' sd. C., probably meaning that their distribution of praise & blame wanted delicacy. C. said, ' S. sd. of my poetry, that I was a Dutch imitator of the Germans.' He sd. he mentioned this, not because he was offended by it, but to show how S. could speak *even* of him.

As to Godwin, C. spoke indignantly of those who from being extravag[an]t admirers became revilers. Tobin was one of these & Montagu another. There is, after all, in G., sd. C., more than I was at one time willing to admit, tho' not so much as his admirers fancied. He himself had declaimed agst. G. openly but visited him notwithstanding. He did not approve of the language of Wordsworth altogether concerning G. On my remarking that I had learned to hate Helvetius & Mirabeau, but retained much of my love for G., the distinction was acquiesced in.

We spoke of national antipathies. C. said, but playfully, ' When I say *a Scotch rascal*, I lay the emphasis on

Scotch, as if the infamy was in that.' C. abused the Irish, but has no dislike to Jews or Turks. This reminds me that I once heard Coler. say : 'When I have been asked to subscribe to a society for converting Jews to Xtnty. I have been accustomed to say, 'I have no money for any Charity, but if I had, I wd. subscribe to make them first good Jews & then it wd. be time to make good Christians of them.'

At this time Hazlitt was in vain striving to become a portrait painter. He had obtained the patronage of Clarkson, who said he had heard he was more able to paint like Titian than any living painter. Someone had said that his portrait of Lamb had a Titianesque air about it, & certainly this is the only painting of H. I ever saw with pleasure. He made a portrait of my brother wh. he knew to be bad & gave up reluctantly. It was destroyed. He painted Mr. Howel's portrait—a strong likeness, but a coarse picture. He was therefore driven to become a writer, & being in this not altogether unsuccessful, he managed to live, but in constant difficulties : hence his morbid views of society, & his *Jacobin* character, as described by Burke at the commencement of his Reflexions on the French Revolution.

26th *April.* With Lamb ; Coler. there. He was violent in his censure of a book by William Taylor of Norwich, wh. has for its second title ' *Who was the Father of Jesus Christ,*' the author's speculative opinion being that Zachariah, the High Priest was the Father. C. contended that such a book ought to be prosecuted for its indecency, it being an insult to the feelings of the community at large. The book exists, & I need give no account of it here. My friend Ant. Robinson admired it & urged Pople to publish it. P. asked my opinion of the publicn. as a mere question of prudence. It was, that without the offensive title, the book might be safely printed. No one would think of it. But if prosecuted, there would be a conviction. The book was never advertised & never read. It is very extravagant & absurd. Roberts (Taylor's biographer) has given me a copy.

On the 6th of June, met Coler. at the Exhibition. He drew my attention to the ' vigorous impotence " of Fuseli, especially in his *Macbeth*. ' The prominent witch,' said C., ' is smelling a stink.' C. spoke of painting as one of the lost arts. Some time after, C., speaking of a great picture by West, said, ' In this picture are a number of figures, each of which is painted as it might have been if it had been a single figure, no one figure having any relation to or influencing any other figure, & tho' they ought to be under each a light of its own, yet each figure looks as if it were in the open-air. He explained the *ideal* beauty to be that wh. is common to all of a class, taking from each individual that wh. is accidental to him.

It was at the same time, the 11th of June, that C. made some strong remarks on a most excellent man whom he professed to admire, even in making strictures that might be thought to depreciate him—Mr. Clarkson. ' I have long,' said C., ' looked on him rather as an abstraction than as an individual who is to be loved because he returns the love men bear to their equals. Clarkson is incapable of loving any except those to whom he has been a benefactor. He is so accustomed to *serve* that he cannot love those whose happiness he can no longer promote. As others are benevolent from vanity, he is made vain by beneficence.' ' Many years ago I called him the moral steam engine, the giant with one idea. I am sorry that the reverence I feel for him as an abstract is in danger of being weakened. The abstract is deteriorating.' This par[ticu]lar remark was occasioned by Cl. having joined the Jacobins in signing a requisition for a reform meeting. This C. cd. not forgive. 12.7.49.

COLERIDGE, WORDSWORTH, LAMB, &c.

I frequently saw Coler. this summer & was made privy to an incident which need no longer be kept a secret. C. was then a contributor to the Courier & wrote an article on the *Duke of York*, which was printed on Friday, the 5th of July. But the Govt. got scent of it & therefore, by the interference of Mr. Arbuthnot of the Treasury, after about 2000 copies had been printed, it was suppressed. This offended C. who would gladly have transferred his services to the *Times*. I spoke abt. him to Walter, but Fraser was then firmly established & no other hand was required for the highest department. I have found a paper in Col.s hand wh. has a reference to this affair. It states what service he was willing to give ; such as attending 6 hrs a day & writing so many articles per week. One paragraph only has any significance, because it shows the state of his mind. "The above, always supposing the paper to be truly independent (1st) of the Administration (2) of the Palace Yard & that its fundamental principle is, the due proportion of political power to Property, joined with the removal of all obstacles to the free circulation & transfer of Property & all artificial facilitations of its natural tendency to accumulate in large & growing masses.'

I met Southey several times this summer. I dined with him once at John Thelwall's in spite of the now wide departure of the poet from the politics of the lecturer, wh. he once himself professed. On the 24th of July, Southey spoke with high admiration of the genius of Blake, both as poet & painter, but deemed him mad. Blake, he said, spoke of his Visions with diffidence as if he did not expect to be believed. S. also spoke of his friend *W. S. Landor* with high admiration, whose *Gebir* is all but a mad poem, but who is not mad in life. Southey spoke with great admiration of Wordsworth but blamed his not publishing his great poem on his own life. ' He has a sort of *miserly*

42

feeling towards his poems as if they would cease to be *his* if they were published.' He praised W.'s pamphlet on the war very highly & allowed but *one* fault in him—that he overrated some of his own poems.

He spoke with feeling of Coler. & his infirmities. With a strong sense of duty he has neglected it in every relation of life.

28th July. An evening at Morgan's, Kensington, where Southey & Coler. were. Coleridge, of Klopstock, said he was a compound of everything bad in Young, Harvey & Richardson. Praised Lamb's *Essay on Hogarth.* He said there were *wrongers* as well as *writers* on subjects. A walk home with Southey alone. Southey on forms of government, said—A republic is in itself the best form of government, as a sundial is the most perfect instrument to ascertain the time of day, but as the Sun will not always shine we have invented clocks. If men had always the sun of reason to enlighten them we should not want artificial forms of government. On *Spain*, Southey was, (as his works show) an enthusiast. He said " A Jacobin revoln. must purify the country before it can come to any good. Catholicism is a bar to all reforms. In the Cortes ₁₀ are bigoted Papists, ₁₀ Jacobin atheists. Of Thelwall he said, "*John* is a very good-hearted man, but a consummate coxcomb. We ought never to forget that he was once as near being hanged as possible & there is great merit in that." He spoke highly of *Blanco White.* He begged me to try & prevent any more articles appearing against him in the Times.

3d of August. Using the word "poor Col.," tho coupled with expression of my admiration, *Lamb* seriously reproved me. " I hate *poor* applied to *such* a man " & referred to a similar sentiment uttered by Ben Jonson of Bacon.

Aug. 7. A chat with Coleridge at Lamb's. I omit an interesting anecdote C. related of his son Hartley, because

43

COLERIDGE, WORDSWORTH, LAMB, &c.

I have sent it to Derwent Col. & it probably will be printed. I can at any time add it. [H. C. R. adds note:—] Vide the Life by Der. Col.

20th Oct. With Col. at Collier's. He spoke both of Scott & Southey as poets in very low terms. Of Scott he said that when you strike out all the interesting *names* of places &c., you will find nothing left. Yet he did not set Southey above him. He spoke of his own poems with seeming disesteem. He publd. his 1st vol. from poverty : he wanted £20. On the first publicn. of his poems he was accused of writing in an inflated & bombastic style ; now he is ranked with those who are accused of a false simplicity. He was asked to repeat from *Christabel* but was unable to recollect the words. This I had witnessed once before.

[There follows a note in shorthand, which reads :—] Both times he was affected by liquor.

[Note added in margin] I heard C. say ' I have been ill with liquor, but I was never intoxicated. Liquor affects my stomach, not my head." Sed quaere.   14.7.49.

1811. *C. Lamb* wrote this year for children a version of the nursery tale of *Prince Dorus*. I mention this because it is not in his collected works, & like 2 vols. of *Poems for Children*, likely to be lost. I this year tried to persuade him to make a new version of the old tale of *Reynard the Fox*. He said he was sure it wd. not succeed. ' Sense for humour,' said L. ' is extinct. No satire but personal satire will succeed.' Many, many years afterwards I prevailed with Sam. Naylor to modernise Reynard, & it has succeeded.   15.7.49.

21 *June*. A pleasant party at Collier's. Lamb in high spirits. One pun from him at least successful. Punsters being abused & the old joke repeated that he who puns will pick a pocket, someone said : Punsters themselves have no pockets. ' No ' said Lamb, they carry only a *ridicule*.   14.7.49.

44

COLERIDGE, WORDSWORTH, LAMB, &c.

Coleridge this winter delivered a course of 15 lectures on Milton & Shakespeare, in Fleet St., wh. I attended. To me they were less interesting than they would otherwise have been, because, having lately been much in his company, the leading ideas were familiar to me. The difference was not great between his conversation, wh. was a sort of lecturing, & soliloquising, & his lectures wh. were colloquial, & in which, as he was himself aware, it was impossible for him to be methodical, & those hearers who enjoyed him most, probably enjoyed most his digressions. The same subjects haunted his mind for many years so that I do not doubt that on comparing my scanty notes with those on Shakesp. publd. lately by Mrs. H. Coleridge, I shd. find a great resemblance. A report of these lectures appeared occasionally in the Morning Chronicle from J. P. Collier. With difficulty I obtained permission from Walter to insert a paragraph in the Times. The only condition of its appearance was that it shd. be cold & dry. Here it is :—" *From a Correspondent.* Mr Coleridge commenced yesterday evening his long announced lectures on the principles of poetry. To those who consider poetry in no other light than as a most *entertaining* species of comp[ositio]n., this Gentleman's mode of enquiring into its principles may want attraction. Unlike most professional critics on works of taste his great object appears to be to exhibit in poetry the principles of moral wisdom & the laws of our intellectual nature, wh. form the basis of social existence. In the introductory lecture delivered last night, Mr. C. deduced the causes of false criticism on works of imagn., from circumstances wh. may hitherto have been thought to stand in no very close connection with our literary habits viz : the excessive stimulus produced by the wonderful political events of the age ;—the facilities afforded to general & indiscriminate reading ; the rage for public speaking & the habit consequently induced of requiring

45

instantaneous intelligibility ; periodical criticism wh. teaches those to fancy they can judge who ought to be content to learn ; the increase of cities wh. has put an end to the old fashioned village-gossiping, & substituted literary small-talk in its place ; & the improved habits of domestic life & higher purity of moral feelings wh. in relation to the drama have produced effects unfavourable to the exertion of poetic talent or of judgment. From such topics it will be seen that Mr. Coleridge is original in his views. On all occasions indeed, he shews himself to be a man who really thinks & feels for himself ; & in the development of his moral philosophy, something may be expected from him very different from critics in general on Shakespeare, Milton & our other national poets. However serious the design of Mr. C's lectures, in the execution he shows himself by no means destitute of the talents of humour, irony & satire."

18*th Nov.* My journal remarks, what indeed I had too often occasion to repeat, that C. was ever referring to what he had done & to what he was to do, & so overlooked what he ought then to have been doing.

24*th Nov.* A visit to C. at Hammersmith with Rough. Today I noticed his antithetical comparn. of the fine arts one with another, quite Schellingian. He incidentally gave to Calderon the fancy & the imagination of Shakespear[e] without his philosophy.

Lecture II. No note.
Lecture III. „   „ [1]   *IV* Ditto.[1]
Lecture V.[2] . . .
Lecture VI.[3] . . .

The 7*th Lecture* my journal praises as incomparably the best, & refers to a report of it which I sent to & which appeared in the Morning Chronicle.

[1] [But *see* Diary *infra*, pp. 114–15.]   [2] [*See* Diary *infra*, p. 115.]
[3] [*See* Diary, p. 115.]

COLERIDGE, WORDSWORTH, LAMB, &c.

Lecture VIII.[1] . . . I lost several lectures going into the country & on my return I renewed my attendance.

In a letter by me to Mrs. Clarkson of the 13th of Decr., I thus characterised these lectures : ' As evidences of splendid talent . . .'[2]   26.7.49.

The concluding lectures were of the same kind & produced the same comment. They were but indifferently attended, & scoffers were not infrequently among the number. Among my personal acquaintance not a few, I always took a lady with me, & among the ladies he had many admirers.[3] . . . One eveng. I saw *Rogers* there, & with him was Lord Byron. He was wrapped up, but I recognised his club-foot & his countenance & general appearance.

Whilst these lectures were going on, Hazlitt too commenced a course on *The History of Eng. Philosophy* at the Russell Institution. 1812. On the 14th of Jan. he commenced & his delivery was so very bad, his lecture being read v. rapidly, & the subject also was so unsuited to a lecture, that tho' the matter was sensible, yet it gave no pleasure, & Stoddart's remonstrances & those of other friends had nearly caused him to break down entirely & give up the course. But he recovered greatly his self-possession & his voice & could read slow[ly] & very much improved, & so he remained an occasional lecturer all his life.

May. At this time appeared in the Quart. Rev. a brutal attack on Lamb in the review of Weber's edition of Ford's works, calling him a *poor maniac*. Barron Field remonstrated with Murray, who protested that he had never heard of Miss L.'s calamity & Gifford, the editor, made the same declaration. The author was [blank in MS.] That C.L. had for an instant only been in confinement was not known to myself or to the rest of C.L.s friends until the

[1] [*See* Diary, p. 118.]   [2] [For quotation, *see* letter, p. 124.]
[3] [*See* Diary, p. 120.]

47

COLERIDGE, WORDSWORTH, LAMB, &c.

recent disclosure in Talfourd's Final Memorials. It was this brutal attack wh. occasioned & justified Lamb's sonnet, *St Crispin to Mr Gifford*, a happy jeu d'esprit.

To this date belongs one of the most felicitous of Coleridge's satirical strokes. His connection with the Courier newspaper & Stuart, its proprietor, is well-known & belongs to C.'s history. The character of Stuart too is well-known. It was after Stuart's desertion of the popular cause & he [*sic* when?] underwent the suspicion of being involved in a famous stock-jobbing forgery of the *Eclair* a French paper that I heard C. praise Stuart warmly. I cd. not help interposing with questions founded on these circumstances. Coler. at length became excited & made a convulsive movement of his lip, preceding the coming joke. ' Why, if I'm pressed as to Dan's strict honesty, which I don't wish to be, I shd. say : Dan's a Scotchman who is content to get rid of the itch when he can afford to wear clean linen. Such men form a class ! "

It was in the month of May that Wordsworth came to London & spent several weeks here. I had now an opportunity of seeing much of him & also of rendering a service both to him & Coleridge, by being mediator between them & healing what at one time threatened to become an incurable wound in their friendship. W. had with very kind intentions, given Basil Montagu a hint of C.'s unfortunate habits which B.M. repeated with unwarrantable exaggerations. The *excess* was denied by W. What he did say was *justified*, & the friends forgave each other.[1] The reconciliation was the easier because, tho' unfriendly words had been uttered by them of each other, yet they were warm admirers of each others genius & most ungrudgingly professed that admiration while, on the contrary, neither of them thought very highly of Southey's

[1] [*See* full excerpts from the Diary of 1812, first printed *infra*, pp. 146–156.]

48

poetical genius, tho' his personal character & his talents as a prose writer & literator [sic] were very highly estimated.

Coler. was at all times a profuse eulogist of Wordsworth's poems but always with qualifications & even with objections to W.'s diction & style, which indeed he has printed. And he was *passionate* in his professions of *love* to him as a man, but these professions expressed but the feeling of the moment. Wordsworth's words might be considered as announcing his permanent convictions. It was delightful to hear Wordsworth speak of himself, when alone with him & he was under no apprehension of being misunderstood & consequently [mis]represented. He said, of wh. I have a note at this very time, that he was convinced he could never make his poems a source of emolument to him & being then independent, he was content. " If men are to become better," he said, " the poems will sooner or later find admirers : If society is not to advance in civilisation it would be wretched selfishness to deplore any want of personal reputation. The approbation of a few compensates for the want of popularity. But no one,' said he, ' has completely understood me—not even Coleridge. He is not happy enough. I am myself one of the happiest of men & no man who lives a life of constant bustle & whose happiness depends on the opinions of others can possibly comprehend the best of my poems."

But W. was loud in his praise of the powers of C.'s mind wh. he said were greater than those of any man he ever knew. From such a man under favourable influences anything might be hoped for. His genius he thought great, but his talents he thought still greater & it is in the union of so much genius with so much talent that he thought C. surpassed all other men. W., in a digression, remarked of himself that he had comparatively but little talent : genius was his peculiar faculty.

49   D

COLERIDGE, WORDSWORTH, LAMB, &c.

If (of which there can be no doubt) genius is properly creation & production from within & talent is the faculty of appropriation from without and assimilation, then Genius & Talent will be given respectively in a larger proportion to Wordsw. & Coleridge.

13th May. A dinner with the Wordsws. at Serjt Roughs. W. S. *Landor* was spoken of. I then knew nothing of him but he was praised by W. for a forthcoming tragedy. Walter Scott was mentioned. W. allowed him little merit, the secret of his popularity lying in the vulgarity of his conceptions which the million can at once comprehend. And of Wilson, whom the Edinb. Rev[iewer]s. had most disingenuously set above Words. W. did not hesitate to say 'Wilson's poems are an attenuation of mine. He owes everythg. to me & this he acknowledges to me in private, but he ought to have said it to the public also.' That this attenuation constituted the merit of Wilson in the eyes of the Edinb. Rev., I have no doubt. Wordsworth's best poems were too highly seasoned with poetry for the Scotch taste. These Reviewers' over-praise of Wilson might therefore be to a degree honest & merely the effect of want of taste, but as the Edin. Rev. was already pledged agst the Lake School, personal ill-will had begun to mix with their want of feeling & they were glad to have an opportunity of conceding all they felt they *must* concede in favour of that school, giving the benefit not to Wordsw. but to his pupil, his imitator & his diluter, (Bar. Field called Wilson '*Wordsworth & Water*') & so obtain credit for candour in admissions which were only another mode of giving effect to ill-will.

I will now anticipate what properly belongs to a later period & say all that I wish to say of *Wilson*. He became after this the editor of Blackwood's Magazine & under his editorship appeared the most contemptuous depreciation of Wordsw. & also very warm praise. I told Wordsw. that it was reported Wilson wrote *all* the articles. W. intimated that he thought Wilson capable of doing so. Tho' Wilson had a residence near Rydal they were never intimate. But there was no open breach between them. Wordsw. related to me—this also I relate by way of anticipation—that when Wilson was a candidate for the professorship of Moral Philosophy in the Univ. of Edinb., Wil. applied to Wordsw. for a testimonial. Words. repeated to me the one he sent—I quote from memory. It imported that if a delicate perception of all the subtleties of Ethics as a science & ability in developing what he thought & making it intelligible & impressing it on others constituted the qualification, he knew no one more highly qualified than Wilson. The testimonial was sent in & Wilson became & I believe, still is, the professor.

I will continue my Anticipation & say here all that occurs to me about the Edin. Rev. wh. I do the more readily because these Reminiscences will probably not be brought down so low as to include what I wish to say.

The scornful treatment of my friends *Wordsw. Lamb* &c &c always incensed me agst the Edin. Rev. W. always tho[ught] that he was robbed of his just fame & consequently of his just emolument by the Edinb. Rev. & many years afterwds he told Serjt. Talfourd that he might say to his friend Mr. Jeffrey that but for *him*, (J.), Wordsw. would have gone to Rome twenty years before he did. Talfourd never reported to W. what J. replied to this. Nor did he to me but he told me this,—That he obtained from J. a frank confession that he was conscious he was wrong in the Judgement he had formed of *Lamb*, whom he *then* admired. But he adhered to his original judgment of Wordsw. & could acquire no taste for him more than he had at first. This is evidenced by the reprinting in the collected papers even of the silly review of the *Rejected Addresses* in wh. the tale of Nancy Lake is declared to be

51

COLERIDGE, WORDSWORTH, LAMB, &c.

' rather a favo[u]rable specimen ' of W. W." I believe no one of the articles on Lamb are [sic] retained.

I once only met Jeffrey by dining with him at Talfourd's. I managed to introduce the subject & obtained from him the strange assertion : ' I was always an admirer of Wordsworth.' ' Indeed,' I answered, " The Edinb. Rev. had a strange way of expressing admiration." But Jeffrey intimated the same sort of thing to Coleridge. Such declarations are worse than foolish.

To go back to this dinner at Rough's. Doctor W[ordsworth]. was there. He & Rough were old College friends, & they retained a regard for each other The Dr. & I sparred about the Bible Society to which he was fiercely & at the same time plausibly opposed. I in vain attempted then, as I have often done since, to urge on High-Churchmen a coalition with Rationalistic Dissenters agt. the Evangelical churchm[en] & the Calvinistic Dissenters. W. W. on the contrary thought the Church had more to fear from the Latitudinarians than from the Methodistic party on the bench of bishops.

The same Eveng. W. accompanied me to Chas. Aiken's where were Mrs Barbauld, all the Aikens & the peculiar friends of the A[iken]s. There was a conscious want of perfect harmony between Wordsw. & the U[nitarian] rational party, as well as the Orthodox party But he gave his hand cordially to James Montgomery & *all* were eager to get near him. The homage was involuntary. He had not then expressed the esteem for Mrs. Barb. wh. he late in life avowed. At this time W. was accustomed to express something like bitterness towards both Mrs. B. & Dr. Aiken on account of their critical Editions of the poets, by which they intercepted, he said, the natural judgments of unaffected readers. This eveng. Wordsw. gave offence by suggesting that possibly Sir Francis Burdett's violent speeches might have suggested to Belling-

52

ham the murdering Percival, saying that when men conceived the idea of committing a horrid act, they tried to conceal the enormity from themselves by fancying a laudable motive. He was rudely opposed by the younger Roscoe. He s[ai]d Sir Fr. B.'s was a constitutional speech. 'What were the people to do who were starving?' "Not murder people," said W., "unless they mean to eat their hearts." He wished to see more of Montgomery & liked Mr. & Mrs. Chas. Aiken. Of the others he said nothing.

At this time Coler. had gone out of his way to attack Mrs. Barbauld in his last lecture in Fleet St.

31st May. An interesting day, being early at Hamond's, Hampstead, where I met Wordsw. & then with a party at Mr. Carr's. Wordsw also there. I abridge from notes. I found W. engaged in defending his own poetry. [This] he was in the habit of doing & this is to be said in justification of his so doing, that he was systematically depreciated in the Edinb. Rev., & the Quart. Rev. either dared not or did not wish to defend him. Talfourd was the first in minor journals to write in his praise & in private circles, individuals, who like myself, were his defenders, became butts of ridicule. He was driven to be his own advocate. At Hamond's was one of the *Millers*, a clergyman (to be mentioned on some other occasion) a cousin of Hamond. He estimated W.'s poems chiefly for the purity of their moral. W. on the other hand, valued them only according to the powers of mind they presupposed in the writer or excited in the hearer. He spoke with contempt of Campbell & analysed with effect the celebrated passage in *The Pleasures of Hope,* "Where Andes, Giant of the Western Star" declaring it to be a jumble of discordant images, which, like Gray's ridiculous image of the Bard's beard, 'streaming like a Meteor in the troubled air' had been stolen without effect from a line by Milton in wh. a spear is for its brightness compared to a Meteor.

53

W. also expatiated on his fears lest a social war would arise between the poor & the rich, and [sic] the danger of which is aggravated by the vast extension of the manufacturing system. This was a topic wh. at this time haunted alike both Wordsw. & Southey. Now that 36 years have elapsed not only the danger has increased but the war has actually broken out & as an evidence that men now distinctly perceive the fact, in France a word has been applied, not invented, wh. expresses by implication the fact. Society is divided into *proprietaires* & *proletaires*. And here we have an incessant controversy carried on by our political economists who discuss the respective claims of *labour* & of *capital*. Hamond urged that the masters would keep Servants in order, but agst this it was remarked that the extent to wh. manufactures were carried was such as to destroy the ancient personal influence of Master over Servant.

Words. also defended earnestly the Church Establishment & was not disconcerted by a laugh raised agst him because having before said he wd. shed his blood for the Church, he confessed that he could not say *when* he had been in a church in his own country. ' All our ministers are so vile.' The mischief of allowing the clergy to depend on the caprice of the mob he thought more than outweighed all the evils that arise out of an establishment & in this I agreed with him.

The same day I dined with Wordsw. at Mr. Carr's. Walter Scott & his wife were spoken of, Mrs. W. S. not favourably by either Davy or Wordsw. Joanna Baillie, however, gave her this good word : ' When I visited her I thought I saw a great deal to like : she seemed to look up to & admire her husband. She was obliging to her guests. The children were well-bred & the house in capital order. She had some smart roses in her cap & I did not like her the worse for that.'—Pollock was there, but

54

he was less in harmony with the poet than Burrell. It was said of him by Burrell " he was a hard-headed man, a Senior Wrangler who thought that ev.thg. was to be done by the head alone & without the heart." Yet I ought to add that the sayer of this is now a very old bachelor occupying a 2d. floor in Gray's Inn & he of whom it was said has been the husband of two wives & the father of more than 20 children—mostly alive now. And he is now the Lord Chief Baron.

1812. *4th June.* Wordsw. at this time lent me *Peter Bell* wh. I read in M.S. with great delight, but not without some disapprobation. It contained one passage so very exceptionable that I ventured to beg him to expunge it. He said : ' Lady Beaumont has advised me to leave it out too. I will see whether I ought not to leave it out. When it did at last appear,—I was abroad at the time—I read a contemptuous rev[iew] in the Times with no other extract than this same passage, the very worst to my taste that ever Wordsworth wrote. It is now expunged & therefore may not be known to the next generation of Wordsworth's readers. Its place is supplied by a picture as wild but not as ridiculous. I will copy it as an illustration of what a man who lives much alone & feeds on his own fancies may bring himself to compose. Peter Bell, looking into a pool of water :

A startling sight
Meets him beneath the shadowy trees.
Is it a fiend that to a stake
Of fire his desperate self is tethering?
Etc., etc.

Is it a party in a parlour
Crammed just as they on earth were crammed,
Some sipping punch, some sipping tea,
But as you by their faces see
All silent and all damned ?

55

COLERIDGE, WORDSWORTH, LAMB, &c.

Mrs. Bas[il] Montagu told me that she had no doubt she suggested this image to W. by relating to him an anecdote. A person walking in a friend's garden, looking in at a window, saw a company of ladies sitting near the window with countenances *fixed*. In an instant he was aware of their condition & broke the window. He saved them from incipient suffocation.

Lamb did not object to this rejected stanza. He said : ' It is full of imagn.' No doubt of that, & what if it were ? But tho' he did not object to that passage, he disliked the whole poem. He saw nothing good in it : he objected that the narrative is slow. My journal adds : ' as if that were not the *art* of the poet.' I might have said that to object to the poet a want of progress is as absurd as to object to the dancer that he does not get on. In both alike the object is to give delight by not getting on.

6th June. I had the satisfaction of introduc[in]g W. to my friend *Ant. Robinson* & of perceiving that they duly appreciated each other. W. had been pleased with a letter by Ant. Robinson on his *Convention of Cintra*, who, he said, had better understood him than I had in my review of it in the *London Review.* This honesty in W. pleased me.

On an earlier eveng. spent with W. at Morgan's with whom Coler[idge] lived, W. eulogised Burns for his poetical apology for drunkenness in his introduction to *Tam O'Shanter.* He also praised the conclusion of *Death & Dr. Hornbrook,* wh. he compared with the abrupt termination of the conflict between Gabriel & Satan in Milton. My journal adds : This remark did not bring its own evidence with it.

During this time Coler. delivered a course of 5 lectures on poetry &c at Willis's Rooms—a mere genteel audience, of course. I heard them all. They suggested little or no observation.

56

Coler. was sadly annoyed by the necessity of thus appealing to the kindness of his friends. He at this time repeated to me an epigram of wh. I recollect only the point. ' I fell asleep & I fancied I was surrounded by my friends who made me marvellous fine promises. I awoke & found these promises as much a dream as if they had been actually made.'

11th June. An unexpected call from W. He had received the information of the death of a dau[ghte]r (Catharine) of the age of 4 & he was going down immediately to Wales to Mrs. W. He seemed deeply affected. I called with him on a Mr. De Quincey, a friend who had been lately in Westmoreland & was much attached to the little child. De Qu. burst into tears on seeing Mr. W. as if *he* had been the father. Miss Wordsw. had written to him. This was the first time I had seen De Qu. I had heard of him only as a literary friend of W. of whose talents as a writer W. thought highly. He has since acquired celebrity as the *Opium Eater* & has lived a sad example of the wretchedness that attends the life of a man of superior intellect whose conduct is the sport of ill-regulated passions. His history is a curious one. He was the son of a widow lady at Bristol who may, for aught I know, be still living—a lady of fortune. De Qu. had, I believe, an independent income, at least he was brought up to no profession & after he left Oxford devoted himself passionately to literature. He became an ardent admirer of the Lake poets in his youth & Cottle has in his *Memoirs* related how, when De Quincey was very young, he enquired of C[ottle] whether Coleridge was not, (as he suspected) very poor, & whether £300 would not be acceptable to him & gave the money on an affirmative answer to these questions.

Here I will digressively state that when Cottle was preparing his *Memoirs* for the press he was requested by

Coleridge's friends to withhold this fact from the public, because it was thght. De Q. had by his subsequent conduct cancelled the obligation. Cottle referring the question to me, I was decidedly of opinion that the fact ought not to be withheld.—De Q. took a residence near Grasmere where he became intimate with the poets. Here I formed an acquaintance with him. While residing here De Qu. became connected with the daughter of a Statesman, a small freeholder—so they are called in the Northern Counties.—It was not till after he had had several children by her, & that to the knowledge of the whole neighbour-hood, that he married her. When this marriage took place he expected that Mrs. Wordsworth & the other ladies of W.'s house would visit her. This they declined doing & in consequence De Quincey's friendship turned to gall & from being the enthusiastic follower, he became the enemy of W., depreciating his works & in his writings, where he could not but praise the poet, he reviled the man. Living without any profitable occupation & unable to convert literature into a means of subsistence, he sank into poverty & drew down the worthy family of his poor wife into his own abyss of misery. They looked up to him as a *Gentle-man* & he made his father-in-law sell his little estate for his benefit & father & family were brought literally to the parish.

I cannot follow his history in all its details. I used occasionally to see him in London. For some years I was the depository of a large collection of books which were kept in my chambers to save warehouse rent, till they were sold to supply his wants. They were classical works & I believe of value. His *Confessions of an Opium Eater* ac-quired celebrity, but it is the only work of his which did. He became an unsuccessful hanger-on [of] the booksellers & took up his residence in Scotland : in London he c[oul]d not possibly maintain himself. I saw him occasion-ally there as a shiftless man. He had a wretchedly invalid countenance : his skin looked like mother-of-pearl. He had a very delicate hand & a voice more soft than a woman's, but his conversation was highly intelligent & interesting. He was *near* being a very attractive man, as he was always an object of compassion. I have not seen him for many years & as a writer, it is only in periodicals that I am acquainted with him. He wore out the patience of Blackwood & of the Edinb. Rev., obtaining from the publishers prepayment for papers wh., being paid for, were not to be had. It has been latterly only in *Tait's Magazine* that I have read his papers, & Tait, I hear, never pays till he has the article in hand. Those wh. I have read with most interest have been the papers entitled "*Autobiography of the Opium Eater*, & these are rendered entertaining because they are full of anecdotes of the great poets of the Lakes. But to create this interest, he has had recourse to the most unworthy expedients. Outraging all decency, he betrays private confidence without the slightest scruple, relating the most confidential conversations, even reporting the unkind words uttered by one friend of another & utterly regardless of all delicacy. I was with Wordsw. one day when the advertisement of one of his papers was read. He said with great earnestness : ' I beg that no friend of mine will ever tell me a word of the contents of those papers ' & I dare say he was substantially obeyed. It was a year or two afterw[ard]s (for these papers went on for a long time & were very amusing) however, that I ventured to say : ' I cannot help telling one thing De Q. says in his last number in [these] very words—that Mrs. W. is a better wife than you deserve. ' Did he say that ? ' W. exclaimed in a tone of unusual vehemence, ' Did he say that ? That is *so* true that I can forgive him almost anything else he says.' Yet writing of Mrs. W. in terms of the most extravagant eulogy, he could not refrain from concluding : ' *But she squints.*'

59

COLERIDGE, WORDSWORTH, LAMB, &c.

Materials of this kind must be limited & local & temporary politics also will fail & therefore I have not been surprised when I have heard anecdotes of the extreme distress to wh. De Qu. has been reduced. It has been such, & at the same time so little confidence has been felt in his management of money that I have heard that Wilson, Jeffrey & other of the literary aristocracy of Edinburgh have been accustomed to send joints of meat & other articles for the house. By this time probably his children have been provided for by her [their ?] relations & I have heard that his eldest daughter has proved a very clever & also morally a well-conducted person & yet of this same girl I heard an anecdote related which, if correct in all its parts, would have made one tremble at the thought of what she would become. *Many* years ago I heard Captain Hamilton relate this story : One day when this child was so young that no one could think her capable of understanding what was said, two sheriff's officers came into the room in wh. her father was, & one of them presenting a writ said : ' I arrest you, Sir.' De Qu. took the writ & said coolly : ' Oh, you are mistaken, Sir. This writ is against my brother. My name is Charles, not Thomas.' The men said he was called Thomas by ev. one, but De Q. was confident. So one of them stept out into the kitchen to the servant. ' What's your master's name, Betty ? ' ' Charles, Sir,' with a curtsey. The little girl had slipped out of the room & told her to say so if she should be asked by either of the men. One is glad to repeat that she is now said to be highly esteemed.   27.7.49.

Aug. 4th. From Mrs. Morgan &c. with whom Coleridge then lived I heard some anecdotes related of his childhood wh. are worth comparing with the printed accounts. ' His father was a clergyman at Ottery St. Mary's, Devon. & he had pupils. On his death Buller, who was probably already a judge ? & who had been a pupil of C.'s father, went to see the widow & made an offer of his patronage for the youngest child, Samuel. He was in consequence taken to London & it was expected he would have a presentation to the Charterhouse. He was however sent by Buller to the Blue Coat School. His family were proud & considered this a degradation. They refused to notice the boy in the school. His brothers would not let him go to them in his school-dress & he refused to go in any other even when he might have gone. He used to dine with Buller on the Sundays, but one day there being company, the Blue Coat boy was sent to dine at the Second Table, & though but *nine* years old he would not go again. Thus he lost his only friend & having no one to shew him any kindness, his childhood passed away in wretchedness. This made him a good scholar, for he had always his book in hand, that he might forget his misery.'

Copied from my journal.

1 3*th Augt.* A long tête-à-tête with Coleridge wh. I availed myself of by shewing him some new scenes to *Faust* & endeavouring to infuse into him a higher & juster sense of Goethe's pre-eminence. I succeeded but partially. He was not pleased with the first scenes in Faust & objected that Mephistofeles is not a Character. I urged that Meph. was not intended to be a character. He is the representative of the human race or rather an abstraction of certain qualities in man & to this he had no reply. He deemed *Mahomet's Gesang* an imitation of Stolberg's *Felsenstrom.* But what is the allegory or import of the *Felsenstrom ?* He was not however offended by *the Prologue in Heaven* to *Faust* tho' a parody on Job. He said of Job : " This incomparable poem has been absurdly interpreted. Job far from being the most patient was the most impatient of men. He was rewarded for his impatience. His integrity & sincerity had their recompense because he was superior to the hypocrisy of his friends."

61

COLERIDGE, WORDSWORTH, LAMB, &c.

Coler : praised *Wallenstein* but imputed to Schiller a sort of *Ventriloquism* in poetry. Wordsworth's *Ruth*, said Col:, has the same fault as it stands now, tho' originally W. had not put sentiments into the mouth of the Lover wh. are now there & wh. would better become the poet. He praised Schelling more than he had done before ; said ' he appears greatest in his last work on *Freiheit*, tho' *his* is the philosophy of Jakob Böhme."

He had been reading *Lear* again. The Fool he thought unlike all Sh's other Fools ; one of the profoundest & most astonishing of all his characters.

20th Augt. Another evening with Coleridge at Capt. Burney's. I copy as a statem[en]t of my own impression what I wrote in my journal—not that I think my impressions either true or valuable :—" He afterwards made many remarks on the doctrine of the Trinity from which I could gather only that he was very desirous to be orthodox, to indulge in all the subtleties & refinements of metaphysics & yet conform with the popular religion. That he is consciously excited by any unworthy suggestion or grossly insincere I do not believe, but that he deceives himself. He repeated a droll poem by himself founded on the raising of devils by repeating formularies of Hebrew words. He considered the most plausible objection to Christianity to be that there is an unfulfilled prophecy in Christ's not having appeared among the Jews, wh. the early Christians expected. But this too may be answered.

Nov. 3d. Col. commenced a course of lectures on Belles Lettres at the Surrey Institution and [sic] which were continued down to the 26th of January. As the novelty of these lectures had worn off & I was familiar with his opinions ; they attracted less attention from me, or I was become more lazy for I have made very few remarks on them. The audience at the Russell Institution were much more evangelical than at the other lecture rooms & some-

COLERIDGE, WORDSWORTH, LAMB, &c.

times C[oleridge] flattered the religious opinions of his
hearers & at other times ran counter to them.[1] Almost
the only note I made on this course of lectures was the
following :—

1813 *Jan. 26th.* Heard Col's concluding lecture.[2] . .
28.7.49.

On the 23d. of January was performed Coleridge's
Remorse, the single drama which he was able to introduce
on the stage. It was with great difficulty that he succeeded in having it performed at Drury Lane. He complained of ill-treatment from Sheridan who slandered it in
Company. He told me that Sheridan had said that in the
original copy there was in the famous Cave Scene :—

Drip, drip, drip ! there's nothing here but dripping.

However there was every disposition to do justice to it on
the stage, nor were the public unfavo[u]rably disposed towards it.[3] . . . It would be out of place in me to play the
critic, nor need much be said. It would be acknowledged
by the friends & enemies of Col. that the poetical merits of
this play are greater than its dramatic merits & for this
very palpable cause, that his poetical mind is as undrama-
tical as Wordsworth's & Lord Byron's. . . .

1813. I saw but little either of Coleridge or any of the
poets &c. this year. I was honestly trying to become a lawyer.

On the 2d. of Feby. I accompanied Aders to see
Coleridge. He spoke of Goethe with more favour than
usual to my German friend. Without meaning to impute
insincerity to C. I may observe that he had a need of
sympathy & therefore preferably said what he knew would
please, not what would displease. He was not a good
disputant. He said that if he seemed to depreciate Goethe

[1] [Not quite accurate. See *infra,* Diary, pp. 135–137.]
[2] [Quotation from Diary *infra,* p. 137.]
[3] [*See* Diary, Dec. 23rd, 1813, *infra,* p. 136.]

it was because he compared him with the greatest of poets ; that he tho[ugh]t Goethe had from a sort of caprice under-rated the talent which in his youth he had so eminently displayed in his *Werter*, that of exhibiting men in a state of exalted sensibility. In after life he delighted in repre-senting objects of pure beauty not objects of desire & passion—rather as statues or paintings. Therefore he called Goethe *picturesque*.

Lessing's *Laocoon* he declared to be unequal, in parts contradictory, his examples destroying his theory.

Reinecke Fuchs. The moral of this piece is that if there be a conflict between dull, blundering knaves such as Isegrim & Bruin, the Wolf & the Bear & a complete, clever scoundrel like Reynard the Fox, Reynard is entitled to victory. It is the prize due to his talents & poor im-becile creatures like the hare & the hens must perish, & as this is the constitution of nature, they do not excite our sympathy. My journal adds : " I never before heard him argue in favour of Buonaparte." He accused Schlegel of one-sidedness in his excessive admiration of Shakespeare.

29th April. Even my visits to Lamb were become rare. This evening I was there & with *Hazlitt*, whose recent appointmt. as a Reporter on the Chronicle paper placed him, as he flattered himself, in a state of ease. The neces-saries of life were supplied to him.

Poets are accused of being insensible to each other's merits. Hamond 1*8th Oct*. told me to-day that he had seen a letter from Walter Scott stating that he had declined the laureateship in favour of Southey,[1] saying : " I am the more popular now, but posterity will enquire most abt. Southey." And Southey showed the same freedom from jealousy towards Wordsworth. He told Hamond that

[1] It ought to be added that the Life of Walter Scott by his son-in-law discloses if not double-dealing, at least " double sentiments " in this matter, not honourable to the great romancer. [H.C.R.]

COLERIDGE, WORDSWORTH, LAMB, &c.

The Recluse was to be published this season & that it wd. establish Wordsworth as the first poet of his age & country. W.'s *Excursion* did appear, but instead of the critical world acknowledging its merits, the Edin. Rev. wrote its most scornful review. " This will never do " was its dictatorial commencement.

30th Dec. with Lamb, Hazlitt &c at Rickman's. *Rickman* produced one of Chatterton's forgeries. In one M.S. there were seventeen kinds of little *ee's*. " This must be modern " said Lamb, " & written by one of the Mob of Gentlemen who write with ease." 3.8.49.

1814. This year also is nearly a blank as concerns the poets ; none of them did I see except Lamb, & with him my meetings were become seldom. His card-parties were held but once a month. I had however the gratification of making the Lambs known to the Aikens & the consequences were that I substituted in the place of disrespect, kindness on the part of Lamb towards the Aikens & the Aikens made known their admiration. This evening we spent at Dr. Aiken's. C. Lamb was infinitely amusing, telling a droll story of an India House clerk accused of eating man's flesh & remarking that among cannibals those who rejected the favourite dish would be called Misanthropists.

Of those I consider as the appendages to the poets I also saw but little. In February De Quincey came to London, but I found his company wearisome. He appeared to me then to be the mere admirer of Wordsw. having nothing of his own, in wh. I did him wrong. But he was certainly cold & dry & wanted all power of conversation. I saw Hazlitt a little. He was put into spirits by being allowed to write in the Edinb. Rev. thro' the introduction of Lady Mac[k]intosh, after having been, as he fancied, ungratefully & insolently dismissed from the Chronicle by Perry.

He printed afterwards in some fugitive paper, that Walter **was** the only newspaper proprietor who treated his writers **as** gentlemen. Perry, he complained to me, treated them as menials.

The publication of *The Excursion* this year was an epoch in Wordsworth's literary life, but suggests nothing here.

25.9.49.

1816. This year my personal acquaintance with Wordsworth & Southey was improved by a journey in the North. I lament to perceive that as my means of knowledge advance, my power of profiting by those means seems to decline. Is it that my curiosity being blunted, I became inattentive or that I had less to note down because I was already familiar with what was said ? It was in Septr. that I went to Mr Wordsworth, introducing to him young Torlonia, the son of the rich Roman banker, & his travelling tutor Mr. Walter, & Mr W[ordsworth] delighted in pointing out the beauties of his home & neighbourhood to the strangers. I was on this occasion impressed by the enviable state of his family & of his circumstances, his distributorship of the stamps relieving him from all anxiety abt. their present support tho' not their future welfare.

On the 9th of Septr. I introduced my companions to the Laureat[e]. A pleasant eveng. with him, Nash, Westall junr., Mrs. S[outhey] & her 2 sisters, Miss Barker &c. Our conversation on politics was very sad. Southey while he confessed that Ferdinand VII wanted generosity, nevertheless asserted that in his severe measures he acted *defensively*. Under the constitution the reformers proposed, he wd. have been at once dethroned.

In England & indeed all Europe, he anticipated a *servile war* & he expected a convulsion in 3 years. I deemed him then as I now believe he was, an honest alarmist. My diary describes Hartley Coleridge as a foreign Jew boy. Coleridge's daughter I was much pleased with. Of the three sisters, Mrs. Coleridge was the least agreeable.

On the 11th of Septr. I set out with Mr. Wordsw. from Keswick on a business journey, he having, as Executor to his brother the lawyer, to sell some of his property. We went first to *Cockermouth*. He rode & I walked. To render some of his poems intelligible, he related the occasion of their composition. I shd. be tempted to state some of these, but I will wait for the Life in which a collection of such notes is to appear. I will compare the future vol[ume] with my diary of the journey, p. 33.

At Cockermouth I had a singular illustration of the *maxim* 'A prophet is without honour in his own country.' Mr. Hutton the solicitor employed to sell some houses, a very gentlemanly & seemingly intelligent man, asked me once : 'Is it true,—as I have heard it reported—that Mr. W. ever wrote any verses ? ' I accompanied W. to *Calder*bridge & *Ravenglass* &c.

I saw Southey again & we renewed our political conversation The point on wh. Southey & Wordsworth differed most was on the law of the Press. S. wd. have punished a second political libel with transportation. W[ordsworth] was unwilling to restrain the press.

On this journey I saw several times *De Quincey*. He was already become the bitter enemy of Words : & for no better reason, as far as I cd. perceive, than that the Ws. wd. not shelter by their patronage, the woman he had married after he had disgraced her, as I have already said. On this journey I became tired of his company, & I regretted having accepted of his hospitality as he had a claim of a return. I had no doubt that De Qu. felt in like manner tired of me & all cordiality between us from that time ceased. This did not of course prevent his making troublesome applications to me when he sunk into absolute poverty, but in that state men care not of whom they

COLERIDGE, WORDSWORTH, LAMB, &c.

borrow or beg. De Qu. tho' he spoke with obvious dislike of Wordsw. as a man, & vehemently agst. Coler : yet eulogised their genius. Of Southey he spoke lowly as a poet. Indeed he appeared to be a sort of Pococurante, abusing all the German great men, *Goethe*, *Schiller*, &c.— Tho' intimate with Wilson he did not praise his poetry.

28.2.51.

During this year my acquaintance continued with Godwin but I was brought to a more close observation of his character as developed under the sad circumstances into which he was brought by imprudence if not recklessness. Early in the year he had visited Wordsworth & left him with feelings of great bitterness. Their diverging political affections separated them. Wordsworth perhaps carried too far his forbearance of the renewed abuses & corruptions of the restored Monarchs, because he thought any evil they could inflict under a domestic government would be slight compared with the utter slavery which would have prevailed over Europe had Buonaparte ultimately triumphed, while such men as *Godwin* & *Hazlitt* were ready to love Buonaparte as the enemy of their enemies. My diary of May 28. 1816. has this paragraph :— " Europe was rising morally & intellectually when the French Revolution after promising to advance the world rapidly in its progress towards perfection, suddenly, by the woeful turn it took, threw the age back in its expectations, almost in its wishes, till at last from alarm & anxiety, even zealous reformers were glad to compromise the cause of freedom & purchase national independence & political liberty at the expense of civil liberty in France, in Italy & most intensely did I rejoice at the counter-revolution. I had also rejoiced when a boy at the Revolution & am ashamed of neither sentiment & I shall not be ashamed tho' the Bourbon shd. become as vile as any of the sovereigns wh. France was cursed with under the ancestors of Louis XVIII ; & tho' the promises of liberty made to the Germans by their Sovereigns shd. all be broken & tho' Italy & Spain shd. relapse into the deepest horrors of papal superstition. To rejoice in immediate good is permitted to us. The immediate is often alone our scope of action & observation."—I then thought that my friends in general erred either in loving or hating too indiscriminately the then objects of their political attachment or antipathy.

It was during this year, Dec. 15, 1816, that *Shelley* attached himself to *Mary Godwin* which led to events that acquired a sad & memorable notoriety. Mrs. Godwin consulted me on the state in wh. Shelley then (Dec. 25th) was with both his wife & the Godwin family. Mrs. Godwin accused Mrs. Shelley of being guilty of adultery & alleged this as an excuse for S.'s conduct. I had no confidence in Mrs. G.'s veracity, nor on her word alone could I believe that Mrs S. was enceinte when she was found drowned by an act of suicide. I learned that all the children of Godwin & Mrs. G. justified the conduct of Mary G. in eloping with Shelley, but I believe Godwin himself did not sanction the act & that it grieved him. But he was under too great pecuniary obligations to Shelley to be able to interfere vigorously.

A few weeks before this was written the death of Mrs Shelley was announced. She was a woman of great ability. Wordsworth especially admired her taste in poetry. He praised her Lives of the Italian poets in the Cabinet Library.

During this year Coleridge was residing with Gil[l]man at Highgate who had generously taken him under his charge. I used now & then to go and see him at Gil[l]man's but I went seldom for I thought the Gil[l]mans treated me with rudeness & this happened to Lamb also. On the 14th of July I took Ch. Becher to see C. when Coler. amused me by declaring that he had years before Goethe discovered his theory of colours, wh. by diverting his attention to other subjects, Southey had prevented his publishing. And on my intimating that I had heard that others had lately announced a like system, C. naïvely remarked that he was very free in communicating his thoughts in conversation. It was this day that Lamb joined us & Gil[l]man came in & assumed an air as if he meant it to express : "Now Gentlemen, it is time for you to go." We took the hint & went & Lamb said he would never call again.

On the 21st of Decr. I accompanied Cargill to Coleridge when we found he had been very ill, but he was able to expatiate eloquently on the distinction bet. fancy & imagination. Fancy he called memory without judgement. See his Lay Sermon. He spoke of German literature ; praised Steffens & lamented the Romanism of the Schlegels & Tieck. He spoke of Hazlitt's attacks on him with unexpected moderation but complained of Lamb's toleration of him, to whom Hazlitt was indebted for what had been thought original ideas in him, & who violated private confidence so outrageously. He was pleased at being told that H. had been knocked down lately by John Lamb, Charles L.'s brother.

I heard Mary Lamb say, after I had cut him for a cause I will now state : 'You are rich in friends. We cannot afford to cast off our friends because they are not all we wish,' & I have heard Lamb say : 'Hazlitt does bad actions without being a bad man.'

It was on Sunday, the 22d of Dec., the day after this conversation with Coleridge, that I broke altogether with Hazlitt. I had read in the morning's *Examiner*, a paper, manifestly by H., abusing Wordsworth for his writings in favour of the King, I rather think especially the sonnet express[in]g the wish that the king could be restored for an instant to his faculties in order to be aware of the victory

COLERIDGE, WORDSWORTH, LAMB, &c.

gained by the nation over Buonaparte. " I recollected,"
he said,—(I quote from memory)—" hearing this gent[le-
man] say ' I shd. wish to see every member of the Ho[use]
of Commons hanged.' I put in a word in favour of Cha.
Fox & Sheridan. But he said : no. There is not one of
them fit to live. And then he referred to what he called
their tergiversation." This eveng I took tea at Basil
Montagu's. Hazlitt on coming in, offered me his hand
wh. I refused. And during the evening I took an opportunity to say : Nothing shd. induce me to continue an
acquaintance with the writer of an article in to-day's
Examiner. Hazlitt said coolly : I am not in the habit of
defending everything I write. I do not say that all I have
written is just. And on my especially remarking on the
breach of confidence, he said : It may be indelicate, but
I must write an article every week, & I have not time to be
delicate. On which I repeated the anecdote of the French
minister to the libeller : Je n'en vois pas la necessité.'
He then made a distinction : I would never take advantage of a slip in a man's conversation, who might say *once*
what was not his real habitual opinion & a repetition
would be a substantial falsehood. But what I published
was an often repeated sentiment, not said to me alone
but many. And such things might be repeated. I replied : One aggravation is wanting in this case & your
vindication amounts to this : ' Tho' I won't lye, I will
betray.' He said he thought it useful to expose persons
who would otherwise gain credit by canting. I admitted
that the attack on Southey's *Carmen Nuptiale* was un-
exceptionable & he said he still believed Southey was an
honest man.

After this evening I never to my recollection exchanged
a word with Hazlitt. I often met him at Lamb's but we
never spoke. He lived 12 years afterwards & many years
before his death he said to Mary Lamb : ' Robinson cuts

me, but in spite of that I shall always have a kind feeling towards him, for he was the first person that ever found out there was anything in me.' That is true, for when I became acquainted with him at Bury, he was living with his elder brother a miniature painter. And I admired him when no one else thought anythg. of him & before he had printed anythg. but wh. by the bye I have said before.

28.2.51.

1817. In the summer of 1817 Ludwig Tieck, the first of the romantic school of poetry in Germany, came to England. His object was to inspect M.S.S. & rare copies of ancient dramas in our public libraries, it being his boast that he had read every accessible printed drama before & contemporaneous with Shakespeare. He was also desirous of seeing Coleridge, whose reputation both as a poet & critic had reached Germany. On the 24th of June, Mr. Green & I accompanied him to Highgate where Mr. Gil[l]man joined us. C. of course was the talker & L. T. is a good listener. However he did talk & abt. religion. He professed Catholicism, but it was of a harmless kind, for while he said that the people in Catholic countries would be without their religion, he admitted that England owed its greatness to the Reformation & he said that the Catholic system requires Protest[antis]m to keep it in order— precisely what Mrs. Barbauld says of the Church & Dissent. He spoke with great love of Goethe but called the *Prologue to Faust* impious (Goethe to me said : How innocent that is !) T. lamented Goethe's want of religion & said his later works are loquacious. C. read some of his own poems & T. seemed impressed by his eloquence.

On the 29th, I accomp[anie]d T. to Godwin to whom he was very complimentary on account of his works.

Speaking on a future occasion of Coleridge, Tieck said he had herrliche Ideen abt Shakesp[eare] but did not estimate highly his formal criticisms. His conversation he admired & said there was much poetry in *Christabel*. He spoke favourably of Strutt's & Lord Chedworth's remarks on Shakesp:. Of Ben Jonson he praised expecially *The Silent Woman* (wh. he has translated.) *The Fox & The Alchemist, The Devil is an Ass & Bartholomew Fair* perhaps his best. Of German literature he did not speak very favourably. He despised his imitators who had become perhaps more popular than himself, such as *Fouqué*. But *Solger* [?] he praised highly.—I shall have to write of Tieck anno 1829 if these Reminiscences ever reach so far.

In December I had a call from Wordsworth & the ladies. We talked abt. Coleridge who had before consulted with me abt. the expediency of prosecuting the Edin. Magazine for a libel, wh. the Wordsworths agreed with me in thinking inadvisable. The publisher had applied to W. to write in his Magazine & had inserted both eulogistic & abusive articles. W. wrote to him coolly not to trouble himself abt. him, W., as he could make no return in kind.

On the 30th I spent the eveng. at Lamb's where I found two parties congregated round the two poets, but Coler. had a thicker mass than W. C. was rambling in his peculiar way to Monkhouse who listened attentively & Manning, who smiled, as my journal remarks, as if he thought that C. shd. not metaphysicise on what he knew nothing abt. . (probably early in 1851.)

27th Dec. I was gratified to-day by hearing Col. eloquently expatiating on the necessity of protecting Hone for the sake of English law. He derided the lawyer's definition of a libel wh. looks only to tendency & disregards intention. *Tilbrook* related a droll anecdote. *Southey* received a letter from a stranger in Essex, with a fee, requesting him to write an acrostic on the name Rebecca Rankin. He was addressing the lady but had a rival who beat him at verse-making. S. did not send the money back, & distributed the money in buying blankets for some poor women at Keswick.

1818. *17th Feb.* This day attended two courses of lectures on the poets, one from Hazlitt, one from Coleridge. Neither seems to have pleased me. My journal remarks on the recklessness of Hazlitt who, to a party mostly of Saints at the Surrey Institution, was all but obscene in his notice of Prior, quoting his unseemly verses agst. Blackmore, & eulogised Voltaire. Of Coleridge [1] I was led to remark that his mind seemed confined within a narrow circle of ideas, wh. he was ever repeating, but wh. he had not the power of adapting to the popular taste.

On the 24th of Feb. I attended in like manner two lectures from the same men. Hazlitt was so vulgarly abusive of Wordsworth that I lost my temper & hissed & attacked him with a violence I afterwards regretted to the persons near me, tho' I said nothing but the truth. Coleridge confirmed the apprehension that these lectures wd. not add to his fame.

1819. In the year 1819 I either did not see at all or saw to no purpose either of the great poets. My journal does not mention anythg. concerning them except that it notices a very unfavourable judgment of *Peter Bell* by Charles Lamb whose judgment against those he loved might be fairly taken. He loved Wordsworth, tho' not so intensely as Coleridge, but he denied him the faculty of story-telling & he deemed *Peter Bell* one of W.'s poorest works & the *Introduction* childish. I wonder that he did not perceive the exquisite beauty of much in the Introduction.

[1] [See *infra*, Diary, pp. 144, 145.]

COLERIDGE, WORDSWORTH, LAMB, &c.

1820. In the year 1820 I saw much both of Wordsworth & Southey. With W. I took a journey thro'
Switzerland, & I have written a brief notice of that
journey. I was mortified by observing that it records
nothing of W. worth recollecting till I recollected it could
not be otherwise, for we were always in motion & W.'s
mind was devoted exclusively to the observation of the
scenes around him. His *Memorials* shew the objects that
attracted his notice.

Southey I also saw on a particular occasion—the
papers of my poor friend Hamond which were given to
him but wh. he transferred to me. I have in speaking of
Hamond noticed Southey's participation in this sad history,
therefore I shall have but little to say, I expect, of the
poets this year.

9th May. Southey at bk.fast with me & afterwards we
walked together to Wapping on Hamond's business. On
our walk he repeated to me his unpublished hexameters &
he had the power to make them agreeable in recital ;—
less unpleasant by far than his naked opinions. He expressed his regret that the King of France did not on his
second return put to death some 16 marshalls & other
great men by martial law or without any trial whatever.
Public opinion, he said, would justify the violence. He
affirmed that before 20 years the excesses of the popular
writers wd. put an end to every free press in Europe.
Now if time be not of the essence of such predictions,
Southey may be in the right after all, for now after 30
years it looks more likely than ever that what he foretold
will take place.

29th October. Leigh Hunt hardly belongs to this set &
I very seldom saw him at Lamb's, yet I remark in my
journal to-day : "Read the *Indicator* to-day. There is a
spirit of enjoyment in this little book which gives a charm
to it. Hunt is the very opposite of Hazlitt in loving

75

everything. He catches the sunny side of all things &, excepting a few antipathies, mostly abstractions, lo ! everything is beautiful."

Wordsworth was in London a considerable time after our Swiss tour & in good plight. My journal has this note : " 18th Nov. At Monkhouse's to dinner with the Wordsw.s, Lambs, Mr. Kenyon. W. in excellent mood : his improved & improving mildness & tolerance must very much conciliate all who know him."

8th Dec. Read the beginning of Keats's Hyperion. My journal says : " A poem of great promise. There are a wildness, power & originality in this young poet which, if his perilous journey to Italy do not destroy him, promise to place him at the head of the poets of the next generation. Lamb places him next to Wordsworth, not meaning any comparison. They are dissimilar."   (13.8.51)

(6.9.51)

1821. The year 1821 supplies nothing to my recollections of the poets & their literary friends. I was at Ambleside on my return from Scotland, only for a short time, but I was happy to find that with Wordsw. & his family my acquaintance had improved to friendship.

1822. In the Jan. of this year 1822 I first saw Hartley Coleridge. He made on me the impression that he was an unpleasant youth, but endowed with qualities wh. would one day confer distinction. Now I look back on him with admiration & compassion.

In the spring of this year Hazlitt & his wife went into Scotland & Mary Lamb told me for what purpose they went before the act was perpetrated. They are gone, she said, & this was on the 9th of April, in order that Mrs. H. should obtain a divorce by proving adultery agst her husband & then he is to marry the daughter of the house in wh.

76

he lodges ! ! ! In fact Hazlitt did obtain the required divorce, in order to obtain wh. his wife was obliged to swear there was no collusion ! ! ! On his return, the girl refused him. She was the daughter of my old tailor, Walker, & sister of the present Mrs. Robert Roscoe, a very respectable woman. W. Hazlitt made this sad adventure the subject of a little book, the worst he ever wrote, thoroughly bad, *The New Pygmalion*. He afterwards married a widow, for wh. he was liable to transportation, according to the case of The King *v.* Lolly.

Some time after the marriage, John Collier met Hazlitt in the street & wished him joy. " You may well wish me joy," said H. " She has £300 a year & is not so bad neither." But the £300 per annum did not last. His wife became tired of him, & the money being in her own hands & she finding that he had no hold upon him [her ?] left him. H. lived a wretched life & died in extreme poverty. I may hereafter say more about him.

Godwin was this year a source of trouble to me. My early admiration of his works led me to form an acquaintance with him which I regretted but from wh. I did not withdraw till I had suffered largely both substantially & in spirits. His pecuniary distresses seemed to have entirely blunted his moral sense. In the June of this year he lost the benefit he had derived from occupying a house which was the subject of litigation. As two claimed he wd. pay rent to neither & he could not be made to see that there was anythg. wrong in his so doing. He did not refuse from prudence bona fide but he thought he might fairly profit by the litigation. It was a piece of good luck. At last he had to pay arrears of rent, costs of action &c. Being in great want & C. Lamb having lent him £50, I could not refuse him £30. Soon after a subscription was opened. I put down my £30 as an already paid subscription & when I ultimately declined all further intercourse with him, I used in jest to say I owed him £20, as I considered £50 wd. be my ultimate loss. What provoked me to abandon all further participation in his affairs was this—that several hundred pounds having been with difficulty raised to rescue him from prison & the money being paid in the assurance that he was thereby set at liberty, the very next day after the payment he was arrested again. Such a man could not be helped I thought, & it was a relief to me when I had courage to take & keep the resolution & tho' he lived many years afterwards, I did not renew my acquaintance. When this *last* occurrence took place I do not exactly recollect.

Among the worst features of Godwin's mind was an utter insensibility to kindness. He considered all acts of beneficence as a debt to his intellect. On this occasion Walter Scott sent £10 but his name was not to be published. This offended him. Had he not been so severely pressed, he wd. have returned the money & refused to acknowledge the gift, leaving that to the Committee. This indeed I do not censure.

21st Dec. Aders, through me, obtained the acquaintance of Coleridge of wh. he was reasonably vain. This day there was a splendid dinner & C. was the star. He talked freely of Wordsworth. He had not seen the last published works, but he spoke less favourably of the later than he did of the earlier works. He reproached W. with a vulgar attachment to orthodoxy in its literal sense. "The later portions of *The Excursion* are distinguishable from the earlier, & I can," said Col. "from internal evidence separate the one from the other." He accused W. of a disregard to the mechanism of his verse & insinuated a decline of his faculties. This judgment I thought to proceed from a feeling of personal unkindness.

I was more willing to concur in what C. said of Southey. He spoke depreciatingly of Southey's politics, declaring

78

him to be morally an independent, intellectually a dependent man.   15.9.51.

1823. I also introduced to the Aders, the Wordsworths & Lambs as well as Flaxmans. Aders's possession of a fine collection of old pictures & his musical connections & the talents of himself & Mrs. A. enabled them to acquire a large acquaintance, wh. otherwise it wd. have been difficult for them to do. On the 5th of April there was a large musical party in Euston Sq. at wh. Wordsw[orth] & Coleridge were present & I noticed a great diversity in their enjoyment of music. Coleridge's was very lively & openly expressed. Wordsw. sat retired & was silent, with his face covered. Some thought he was asleep. He *might* pass over to sleep after enjoyment. He declared himself highly gratified & indeed came to the party after he had declined the invitation. Flaxman, who was also there, confessed that he could not endure fine music *long* : it exhausted him. So it might be with Wordsworth.

On the *4th of April* I was one of a party at dinner at Monkhouse's, concerning which there is a letter in Talfourd's *Letters of Lamb,*Vol. II p. 95,[1] to Bernard Barton. Lamb says of this party : " I dined in Parnassus with Words., Col :, Rogers & Tom Moore ; half the poetry of England constellated & clustered in Gloucester Place. Coler[idge] was in his finest vein of talk—had all the talk. . . . We did not quaff Hippocrene last night."[2] The short letter is in Lamb's charming style. I have this to add. It is a pity indeed to put water to wine, but there is no help for it. I and Mr. Gil[l]man were the only

[1] [Macdonald gives the letter under the date April 5, 1823.]
[2] Of this dinner an account is given in Moore's *Life*, wh. account is quoted in the *Athenæum* of 23d April, 1823, wh. occasioned my sending a letter wh. appeared in the *Athenæum*. *Post.* 18.8.58. [H.C.R.]

unpoetical men at table besides the Amphitryon. My
journal says : " Our party consisted of W., Col. L.,
M. & R., 5 poets of very unequal worth & most dis-
proportionate popularity whom the public would arrange
probably in the very inverse order except that it wd. place
Moore above Rogers. Coler[idge] alone displayed any of
his peculiar talent. He talked much & well. I have not
for years seen him in such excellent health & spirits.
His subjects, metaphysical criticisms on words. He talked
chiefly to Wordsw[orth]. Rogers occasionally let fall a
remark. Moore seemed conscious of his inferiority. He
was very attentive to Col. but seemed also to relish L.
whom he sat next. L. was in a happy frame : kept himself within bounds & was only cheerful at last." This
seems at variance with his own letter for he complains of
headache & did not go to Aders' party. I have a very distinct recollection of more than I put in my journal, as is
often the case. For instance I can add this with confidence. Lamb sat next Tom Moore & when he was sufficiently touched with wine to be very amusing, I over-
heard him say with a hiccough, ' Mr. Moore, let me drink
a glass of wine with you," suiting the word to the action.
" Hitherto Mr. Moore I have had an antipathy to you ;
but now that I have seen you I shall like you ever after."
Some years after I mentioned this to Moore : he recollected the fact but not Lamb's amusing manner. It occurred to me at the time that Moore felt, if not his inferiority, at least that his talent was of another sort. For
many years he had been the most brilliant man of his
company. In anecdotes, small talk & especially in singing,
he was supreme ; but he was no match for Coleridge in
his vein ; as little could he feel Lamb's humour.

April 4. 1823 [This is a subsequent addition pasted on
the back of pp. 48-55] " Dined at Mr. Monkhouse's, a
gentleman I had never seen before, on Wordsworth's in-

vitation, who lives there whenever he comes to town. A singular party, Coleridge, Rogers, Wordsworth & wife, Charles Lamb, the hero at present of the London Magazine, & his sister (the poor woman who went mad with him in the diligence on the way to Paris) & a Mr. Robinson, one of the minora sidera of this constellation of the Lakes, the host himself, a Mæcenas of the school, contributing nothing but good dinners & silence. Charles Lamb, a clever fellow certainly, but full of villainous & abortive puns which he miscarries of every minute. Some excellent things however have come from him, & his friend Robinson mentioned to me not a bad one. On Robinson's receiving his first brief, he called on Lamb to tell him of it. I suppose, said Lamb, you addressed that line of Milton's [sic] to it : ' Thou first best [great] cause *least* understood.' There follow a number of puns & anecdotes by Coleridge & Lamb."

The Rev[iewers] Athen. April 23. 1853. introduce the above extract with the remark : "The tone of it we do not like " & add at the end that they shd. like to see Lamb's account of the same dinner & after-dinner table-talk."

2d. May. I dined with Coleridge at Mr. Green's in Lincoln's Inn Fields C. was the only talker, but, says my journal " he did not talk his best. He repeated one of his own jokes by wh. he offended a Methodist lady at the whist table by calling for her *last trump* & confessing that though he always thought her an angel, he did not before consider her to be an *arch-angel*."

This year arose the quarrel between Lamb & Southey of which I need say nothing because it is fully stated in the *Letters* of Lamb, among which Lamb's *Elia* letter appears. Southey told me that Lamb had written to him afterwards a letter of deep contrition for that letter. There is nothing more likely than that Lamb shd. express a great deal more sorrow than it was right in him to feel. I may add as to that same Elia letter that I felt flattered by the being singled with the other of Lamb's friends under the initials of my name. I mention it as an anecdote which shows that L.'s reputation was spread even among lawyers, that a 4 guinea brief was brought to me by an attorney, an entire stranger, at the following Assizes by direction of another attorney, also a stranger who knew nothing more of me that that I was Elia's H. C. R. This letter of Lamb's has higher merits in my eyes than any kindness towards me. His praises of Leigh Hunt & Hazlitt were most generous by wh. he wilfully exposed himself to obloquy, & towards Hazlitt especially, because he & Hazlitt were at that time not on friendly terms. Indeed Hazlitt was always putting the friendship of all who knew him to a severe trial, such as few could sustain as well as Lamb—the most kind, generous & self-sacrificing of men.

It is but fair that I shd. add that in Blackwood's Magazine for November there is a humourous attack on Lamb for his letter to Southey, which my journal says " is not ill-done," tho' I could not have been pleased at a note to the passage—" H. C. R. unwearied in every service of a friend "—the note being :—" Correspondent & caricaturist of Wordsworth."   30.10.51.

1824. The year 1824 does not supply many materials to my reminiscences of the poets & that connection.

5th Mar. In March I was at Lamb's with Monkhouse when a religious conversation arose between them. My journal notices the strong anti-religious language of Lamb, & at the same time I am convinced, as it justly remarks, that Lamb was a man of " *natural piety* " & that his supposed anti-religious language was in fact directed solely agst the dogmatism of systematic theology. He has the spirit of devotion in his heart & the organ of theosophy in his skull.

COLERIDGE, WORDSWORTH, LAMB, &c.

The Wordsworths were in London this spring when I saw them frequently with the Lambs, Aders, & Flaxmans, all of whom I had brought together.

19th April at Monkhouse's I met Wordsw[orth] & Ed. Irving together. W. stated that the pressing difficulty on his mind had always been to reconcile the prescience of the Almighty with accountability in man. I stated mine to be the incompatibility of final & absolute evil with the Divine supremacy. Irving did not pretend to answer either objection. He was no metaphysician he said, & knew no more of God than was revealed. This did not meet but evaded the difficulty. The poet he felt to be too great to be angry with & he seemed to take no offence even with me.

3d. June. A large party at Green's, where, in spite of the dancers, Coleridge was willing to metaphysicise. He declaimed this eveng on the growing hypocrisy of the age & the attempt to put down liberality of speculation. Sir Humphrey Davy had joined that party & they were patronising Granville Penn's attack on geology as anti-Christian ! They consider the modern theory of a deluge anti-Mosaic. Where should the dove pick up a leaf ? &c. &c. C. displeased me by speaking bitterly of Schlegel & Ludwig Tieck, abusing Tieck in the style of Schelling. The atheist, said Coleridge, seeks only an infinite cause. The spurious divine is content with a mere personal will which is the death of all reason. The philosophic theologian unites them—but *how*, he did not say. C. declared German philosophy to be in a state of rapid deterioration. When did he write the passages from Schelling published as his own in his Biog. Literaria ?

10th June I went with C. L. to Highgate, self-invited. My journal says " A rich evening at Gil[l]man's. The Greens, Collins R.A., the Aders & a Mr. Taylor, a young man of talents in the Colonial Office." This must have been Henry Taylor, the future author of *Philip van*

83

COLERIDGE, WORDSWORTH, LAMB, &c.

Arteveld, my present acquaintance. Coler., says my journal, "talked his best & his superiority above Irving the more apparent because they seemed to think alike. He dwelt on the internal evidence of Xtnty, insisting on its supplying the wants of our nature. Coler. as his daughter now confesses, holding as of no value, the *historical* evidence of Xtnty. "The Advocatus Diaboli of the eveng. was Mr. Taylor," says my journal, who, if that acct. be correct, with verbal acuteness & in a very gentlemanly tone, but over-confidently, set up Mahomet as enjoying his own internal conviction & as having improved the condition of mankind. Lamb asked him whether he came in a turban or a hat.[1] There was also a Mr. Chance who irritated Irving so that Irving said in anger : Sir, I reject the whole bundle of your opinions ' But I thought Mr. Chance had only words : Irving smelt Antinomianism in them.

Coleridge was unfriendly to the Germans, & called Herder a coxcomb, setting Schiller above Goethe, granting the great poet only the merit of exquisite taste & denying him principle. It requires great modification & great qualification to render this just. There is something of truth in such assertions, but they are more false than true.

Irving on our walk home spoke of a friend who had translated *Wilhelm Meister* & said of him : We do not sympathise on religious sentiment." This was *Carlyle* whom he did not name. But, continued I[rving] 'When I perceive there is a sincere searching after truth, I think I like a person the better for not having found it.' Probably, says my journal, he suspected I was a doubter. On this same walk Lamb spoke of his friend Manning as the most wonderful man he had ever known,—greater than Cole-

[1] [There is a marginal note in Dr. Sadler's hand : " Mr. Field and Mr. Cookson added here, ' When the party were breaking up and the company were severally looking for their hats.' "]

ridge or Wordsworth. Yet he had done nothing, & tho' he travelled in China that produced nothing. Him I knew afterwards—an interesting man, but nothing more.

6th July. Tea at Lamb's. There was a party, Hessey the publisher among them—Giving a somewhat over-done description from De Quincey, the opium-eater's lips, of his sufferings, Lamb remarked that he ought to choose as his publishers *Pain & Fuss* (Payne & Foss, who, by the bye, were not publishers). Clare, the shepherd poet was there, a feeble man, but he was ill, & Elton the translator from the classics, who looked more like a hunter than a poet.

Probably an anecdote belong to *this* year, tho' I have not found it in my journal & have but an imperfect recollection of it. The incident was amusing when it occurred. *Words.* & *Lady Morgan* were invited to dine at I forget whose house. The poet would on no account take her downstairs, & he disturbed the table arrangements by placing himself at the bottom when her ladyship was at the top. She was either unobserving of his conduct or resolved to show him she did not care for it, for she sent the servant to beg him to drink a glass of wine with her. His look was as solemn as if it had been a death summons. This I saw. I was told she asked her neighbour Has not Mr. Words. written some poems ?   26.xi.51.

1825. I did not see any of my north-country friends this year, that is 1825, & therefore this year wd. have been a blank in the annals of my poetically minded friends but for my frequent visits to dear Ch. L   On the 10th of Feb. I saw in Lamb's chambers, says my journal, "a forward, talking young man" introduced to Lamb as his great ad-mirer. "He will be a pleasant man enough when the obtru-siveness of youth is worn away a little." Now this same man, viz Harrison Ainsworth, is the author of numerous popular romances of the class of Spanish Beggar & Bandit tales, constituting the old daily literature. They have been & are still popular tho' of the most mischievous kind, his heroes being generally banditti or highwaymen or political characters of a deplorable notoriety—a man therefore who could not venture to stand a ballot at the Athenæum.

It is barely within the field assigned to this chapter to mention that I this year succeeded in inducing a barrister going to India to take as his clerk a son of John Hazlitt, W. Hazlitt's very inferior brother, which occasioned Talfourd's ill-naturedly telling me that I had more pleasure in serving disagreeable than agreeable people. I do not know what has become of this lad. He was a smart lad & was doing well for a number of years.

An important incident in Lamb's life, tho' in the end not so happy for him as he anticipated, was his obtaining his discharge with a pension of almost £400 a year from the India House. This he announced to me by a note put into my letter box :—" I have left the India House. D— time. I'm all for eternity." He was rather more than 50 years of age. I found him & his sister in high spirits when I called to wish them joy on the 22d of April. " I never saw him so calmly cheerful " says my journal, " as he seemed then." It is notorious this did not last. In the autumn this joy was already somewhat abated when I found the parodist Hone with him, to whom he rendered great kindness by supplying him with articles for his " Every Day Book " wh. are however known to the readers of Lamb—especially his *Selections from the Ancient Dramatists made at the British Museum.* These were afterwards collected & published in two small volumes. I sent these *Selections from the Ancient Dramatists* to Ludw. Tieck. He said of them " Sie sind aus meinem Herzen geschrieben.—They are written out of my heart." The remark was made as well of the criticism as of the text.

16th.2.52.

1826 This too was an unproductive year. The poets from the North did not come to London. My chief correspondence with Wordsworth arose out of his dissatisfaction with his publishers the Longmans, from whom he had obtained scarcely anything in all his life. He had so little acquaintance with the business part of literature that he even applied to one so ignorant as myself to negotiate with a publisher for him. I had neither the acquaintance with persons nor familiarity with business to qualify me for the undertaking, & was therefore of no use to him. On this subject I saw several times Alaric Watts, who had undertaken this for Wordsworth. But ultimately he did nothing, except, I believe in publishing some small pieces in an *Annual* of wh. he was editor. Wordsworth was averse to let anything of his appear in these poor imitations of the German *Musen-Almanachs*, but I believe somethg. of his was so published by A. Watts. I fear that neither poet nor editor was satisfied with the result.

In May I was in company with *Sam : Rogers*, with whom I was becoming acquainted. He praised Wordsworth but lamented his obstinacy in adhering to tasteless peculiarities. There was at this time a current anecdote that Rogers once said to Wordsworth " If you wd. let me edit your poems & give me leave to omit some half dozen & make a few trifling alterations, I wd. engage you shd. be as popular a poet as any living," & that W. answered : ' I am much obliged to you Mr. Rogers ; I am a poor man but I wd. rather remain as I am."

In May I was engaged reading Coleridge's *Aids to Reflexion*, that beautiful *composition*, in the special sense of being compounded of the production of the Scotch Archbishop *Leighton* & himself. I compared it to an ancient statue, said to be made of ivory & gold, likening the portion belonging to the Abp. to the ivory, & that of the poet to the gold. Coler. somewhere admits that, musing over

Leighton's text, he was not always able to distinguish what was properly his own from what was consciously derived from his master. J. J. Taylor quotes this & hints that this might be the case with St. John in his old age when writing his Gospel. On first reading these *Aids*, I remarked that his, Coleridge's philosophy was his own, his religion that of the vulgar. This [is] in my journal. Might I not more truly have said that Col. was not unwilling in one publication to write both *eso*terically & *exo*terically? I also at first considered this as an attempt to express Kantian principles in the English language & adapt it to popular religious sentiment.

15*th June.* With the Montagus & Irving at Highgate. In my journal I wrote " Col. eloquent as usual but I never took a note of his conversation wh. was not a caput mortuum, tho' there was still the sense of a glorious spirit having been active. Irving not brilliant, but gloomy in his denunciatn. of God's vengeance for the irreligion of the country. The only thing he at this time said wh. I heard with satisfaction was his confession that Coleridge had convinced him that he was a Bibliolatrist. Of Irving I have elsewhere written. Coleridge at a later period of his life declared I. to be mad in the juridical use of the word. He had been unsettled by excessive flattery stimulating exorbitant vanity.

1827 was a more entire blank than the preceding as to all personal intercourse with Wordsworth &c. except that I had become a correspondent with Miss Wordsw., his sister, & my letters as well to her as the rest of the family were preserved & returned to me on his death. My short accounts of my journeys were thought good by him from their condensation & some of these may be worth preserving.

1828 This year I became acquainted with *Quillinan,*

who was then the friend & became afterwards the son-in-law of Wordsworth. He was then the friend only of *Dora* Wordsworth to whose care his wife had, at her death, entrusted the educn. of her children in Protestant principles, Qu. being a Catholic & having undertaken on his marriage to bring up his daughters, if any, Protestant. The sons were to be brought up Catholics. He had only daughters. Qu. most scrupulously kept his word, but he informed me not long before his death that his wife was inclined to pass over to the Rom. Cath. Church wh. he wd. not encourage. His attachment to the R. C. Church of wh. he made a boast, was of a very slight texture. By the knavery of Sir Egerton Bridges, his son, & the son's attorney, Qu: was involved in sad litigation by wh. however his character did not suffer except on account of manifest indiscretion, but wh. wd. have made a beggar of him if he had not been a beggar before. W. visited Qu. this year & in the summer I saw him several times. He approved of my leaving the bar & if I had needed to be confirmed in my resolution his approbation wd. have sufficed. I was not a little gratified by hearing that, at Saml. Rogers', he declared me to be the wisest barrister he had ever known.

I may here digressively refer to a very curious note on this subject contained in *W. S. Landor's* " Pericles & Aspasia " in wh. W. S. L. in the midst of a bitter attack on the American *N. P. Willis* reproached him (very absurdly by the bye) for disrespect towards Mr. R.—— who is praised for this same act. In fact W. S. L's well-intended but ill-executed compliment is really more objectionable than the American letter giving an account of a bk.fast in my chambers.

28*th May*. A dinner at Quillinan's who was desirous to gratify some of his military friends with the sight of two poets. He had been a Hussar as was recollected to his disadvantage by a contemptuous critic of his poems in the

COLERIDGE, WORDSWORTH, LAMB, &c.

Athenæum. There was a Colonel Miller, a man of a fine military air without any swagger, who had distinguished himself in the Peruvian army ; *Kenyon*, then designated as the friend of Wordsworth & Southey, an American lady, a Miss Douglas, of whom W. said : ' She is anxious to see famous people & talk herself.' Southey was there, sadly out of humour at the Cath[olic] Emancipation then going on, but restrained by being in the house of a Romanist. During this visit to London, Wordsw. indulged the hope to accompany me to Italy wh. he executed 9 years afterwards when the activity of his mind was abated. He wd. have required the permission of the Govt. He at this time stated that, including a life annuity of £100 from Sir Geo. Beaumont, but subject to the maintenance of his sister, he had £400 per ann independently of his office income.

3d. June Wordsworth brought *Hills* to bk. fast with me. I shd. say, mentioning Hills, that he was a great friend of John Wordsworth & a warm admirer of the poet wh. brought us acquainted. He for a time fluctuated between law & literature. Ultimately he decided in favour of a literary life—that is bookish indolence. He met on a steam-boat a Quaker family & fell in love with the young lady of the party, Wordsworth's poetry being the seductive medium—a pure & idealised *Galiotto*. They married ; he lived abroad where he died also many years ago. He published a metrical translation of *Faust* wh. he gave me, but it acquired no reputation. He was happy in his wife, but used to complain of her family, especially brothers, for having over-reached him in money matters. He used to speak bitterly of Quakers as a body, as if slyness & selfishness were their characteristic qualities.

During this year Lamb & his sister were living on Enfield Green near a small inn. My occasional visits were acceptable to them & I had a bin at the inn. I introduced them to Relph but tho' they & he alike wanted society yet they had too little in common to be companionable. When I went, whatever the hour of the day, Dumbee Whist was resorted to. Lamb had no other occupation than the reading of old books & occasionally writing verse to wh. he was becoming less apt & less inclined. My visits to the Lambs in this their solitude & a few letters between Miss Wordsworth & myself constituted all my intercourse with them before my journey to Italy wh. changed for a time my habits & occupations.

1829 At this time I used to see Moxon in whom C. Lamb took an active interest & whom he induced to marry their adopted child Miss Isola. At this time too, in 1829, I found Lamb anxious to serve Martin Burney, who by his injudicious call to the bar & habits of indulgence had brought himself to a state of great want. Through Rickman & Alsager he was able sometimes to procure employment for Martin, to whom he was attached & who, notwithstanding his infirmities, was an object of tender interest.

COLERIDGE'S LECTURES

THAT Coleridge delivered at least four courses of lectures in London during the winters of 1808, 1811, 1812, and 1818 is well known, as is also the fact that his success as a public lecturer was variable, though it is only from the imperfect and disjointed notes taken by some of his audience, notably J. Payne Collier and H. Crabb Robinson, that the epoch-making criticism of Shakespeare and the later Elizabethan dramatists was put together and ultimately published by Mrs. Henry Coleridge for the first time in 1849.

Among the *Remains of Crabb Robinson* there exist accounts of Coleridge's lectures, criticisms of his method and manner by his friends, and above all the full syllabuses of the courses of 1811, 1812, and 1818, not all of which have hitherto been printed. Crabb Robinson first met Coleridge in private at Charles Lamb's on November 14, 1810, but his interest in the poet had been roused long before. He writes in his *Reminiscences of Coleridge, Wordsworth, Lamb,*[1] *etc.* : " I have a distinct recollection of reading *The Monthly Review* of the first volume of Coleridge's poems (before I went abroad in 1800) and of the delight the extracts gave me, and my friend Mrs. Clarkson [2] having become intimate with him, he became an object of interest with me from my return from Germany in 1805." Mrs. Clarkson suggested that Robinson should advertise Coleridge's lectures among his friends in 1808, and he eagerly responded though he was himself unable to attend them regularly. Coleridge, doubtless at Mrs. Clarkson's request, sent Robinson an order of admission accompanied by the letter which will be found on pp. 28, 29 of this edition of the *Reminiscences.*

Though prevented by his engagements from regular attendance at the lectures, Crabb Robinson diligently took notes

---

[1] [*See* p. 28.]
[2] [The poet was extremely intimate with the wife of the abolitionist, and retained his affection greatly as he disappointed her hopes of him.]

92

COLERIDGE'S LECTURES

whenever he was able to be present. Among his papers there are preserved two pages which summarise Coleridge's lecture on poetry, the second of the course, delivered on February 5, 1808. These have been printed in Sadler's edition of Henry Crabb Robinson's Diary (2 vol. edition, Vol. I, p. 140), but since they are not well known, and since, "detached minutes" though they be, they help to indicate the poet's discursive treatment of his theme, they are reprinted here (pp. 102 *et seq.*).

It appears even from these notes that Coleridge was already apt to range from heaven to earth, from earth to heaven in his public discourses, and one can easily believe that, in spite of his fire and eloquence,[1] his abrupt transitions and numerous digressions were often too much for his audience.

De Quincey's account of this first course of lectures and of the ineffectiveness of the speaker, when he chanced to keep his appointment, is well known. Coleridge was at this time continually under the influence of opium, and his friends might well despair of him and his future. Audience after audience were dismissed " with pleas of illness, and on many of his lecture-days (the speaker is De Quincey) I have seen all Albemarle Street closed by a lock of carriages filled with women of distinction, until the servants of the Institution or their own footmen advanced to the carriage-doors with the intelligence that Mr. Coleridge had been suddenly taken ill."

Coleridge's movements for the next year or two are not very certain. We know that he left London for the Lakes early in 1809, and that he spent most of his time there in Wordsworth's house at Allan Bank near Grasmere. When he returned to London in the summer of 1810 it was in the company of Basil Montagu. Crabb Robinson gives [2] us a pretty full account of the consequent estrangement from Wordsworth, the result of Montagu's repetition and exaggeration of Wordsworth's confi-

---

[1] [He writes to H. C. R. about the lectures of 1808 : " I feel that I have a right to praise, for my Heart on such occasions beats in my Brain."]   [2] See *infra*, pp. 146–156.]

COLERIDGE'S LECTURES

dential warning that Coleridge's habits did not conduce to domestic comfort. Both poets suffered deeply from the misunderstanding, but Coleridge, as was natural in his isolation and well-grounded dissatisfaction with himself and his own failures, far more profoundly than Wordsworth. Coleridge knew himself only too well when he wrote

> To be beloved is all I need,
> And whom I love, I love indeed.
> Frail is my soul, yea, strengthless wholly [1]
> Unequal, restless, melancholy ; [1]

and he never recovered from the shock of Wordsworth's apparent betrayal. The treachery was much more apparent than real, and at worst Wordsworth was guilty of nothing more than imprudence in discussing his friend's shortcomings with such a man as Montagu, but it was natural enough for him to try and spare Montagu the discomfort entailed by Coleridge's presence as a house-mate.

Moreover, Wordsworth, as he himself told Robinson in 1812 à propos of another subject, but before a reconciliation had been effected, was " one of the happiest of men " nor had he Coleridge's cause for self-castigation. He could not guess what agony —the word is no exaggeration—his careless statement caused when repeated with embroideries and without the context. The misunderstanding deepened as time went on, and it was not until May 1812, when Wordsworth was in London, that Crabb Robinson successfully acted as intermediary between the friends and the quarrel was patched up to the infinite satisfaction of both, though it was " never glad confident morning again " for either of them. A full account of the whole affair and of Crabb Robinson's action [2] will be found in the diary for that month (printed

---

[1] [These lines were omitted when the poem was published in 1816.]

[2] [See also Dorothy Wordsworth's Letter to Mrs. Clarkson, May 12, 1812; William Wordsworth's Letters to Mrs. Clarkson, May 6 and June 4, 1812 (Knight: *Letters of the Wordsworth Family*, vol. 2, pp. 3, 4, 8. Nos. 243, 244, 245.)]

for the first time in this volume), and he had every cause for his self-gratulation : " I flatter myself therefore that my pains will not have been lost and that through the interchange of statements which but for me would probably never have been made, a reconciliation will have taken place most desirable and salutary." A week later, on May 19th, he wrote that : " W. has seen C. several times and been much in his company, but they have not yet touched upon the subject of their correspondence. Thus, as I hoped, the wound is healed, but, as I observed to Mrs. C[lark-son] probably the scar remains in Coleridge's bosom." Henry Crabb Robinson was a shrewd observer and student of human nature, and there is little doubt that the famous lines in *Christabel* may be applied to this episode, though it is more likely they originally referred to the quarrel with Southey after the break-up of the Pantisocracy scheme :

> Alas, they had been friends in youth ;
> But whispering tongues can poison truth ;
> And constancy lives in realms above ;
> And life is thorny ; and youth is vain ;
> And to be wroth with one we love
> Doth work like madness in the brain
>   •   •   •   •
> They stood aloof, the scars remaining,
> Like cliffs which had been rent asunder.

But we are anticipating the date of Coleridge's second course of lectures, which were delivered in November 1811, some months after he had left Montagu's house and established himself in that of Mr. John Morgan at 7 Portland Place, Hammersmith, where Crabb Robinson appears to have been a comparatively frequent visitor. Thanks largely to Mr. Morgan, Coleridge this time fulfilled his engagement, and the fifteen lectures were duly delivered. Already on November 6 Coleridge had sent Robinson a prospectus, together with the following letter :

COLERIDGE'S LECTURES

My dear Robinson,

The Coachmakers' Hall having not Literary or philosophical Redolence, or rather smelling somewhat unsavory to the nases intellectuales of all my wealthy acquaintance, partly from past political sporting clubs and partly from th' present assignment to Hops and the instruction of grown gentlemen in Dancing, I have at length procured another Room every way answering my purposes—a spacious handsome room with an academical staircase and the Lecture room itself fitted up in a very grave authentic poetice-phi[losophical]¹ Style, with the Busts of Newton, Milton, Sha[kespeare,]¹ Pope! and Locke behind the Lecturer's Cathedra. I have likewise lowered the prices from 3 and 4 to 2 and 3 guineas. I am sure you will say what you can for me among your Friends but what I more particularly wish you to do is to see it advertised in the *Times*, if by *favor* it can be done so as to *advertise* only as many lines as will not exceed the price of an ordinary advertisement, and to let the rest appear as part of the Paper itself. I certainly should do my best to repay it by sending occasional articles to the Times, prose or verse. Perhaps you may have it in your power to conciliate Mr. Walter's good will towards me in this Business. Likewise do you know any member of the Russell Institution to whom you cd entrust a few Prospectuses to be placed in their Library or Chatting Room ? I have left two or three at the Westminster Library.— At present my Dormitory at least is at Mr. Morgan's, Portland Place, Hammersmith.

I am very anxious to see Schlegel's Werke before the Lectures commence.

> May God bless you, my dear Sir,
> and Your sincere Friend,
> S. T. COLERIDGE.

¹ [Torn by Seal.]

96

HENRY CRABB ROBINSON

*From an engraving after a pencil sketch from life, September 4th,
1860, at the Athenaeum Club, by G. Scharf, F.S.A.*

COLERIDGE'S LECTURES

[As usual, Robinson took an infinity of trouble to assist a friend, and his diary for the month is full of references to his efforts.

Thus :—]

Nov. 7 . . . Afternoon wrote . . . to Coleridge about prospectuses for his lectures . . .

Nov. 14 . . . Walked into City to distribute Coleridge's bills . . . Chatted a little with C. Lamb, who expressed himself morally concerning both Willm. Hazlitt and S. T. Coleridge and their habits. I had afterwards occasion to write to Coleridge and I was made low-spirited by the reflection which attending to the concerns of such a man naturally awoke. That a man of preëminent talents should be reduced to the necessity of soliciting for guineas and even for dollars is a most painful thing to see . . .

Monday, 18. . . . With Walter to request he would put in a paragraph for Coleridge this evening. He hesitated, and I was hurt. He consented, not with good grace, and after the lecture I sent an article [*see* pp. 45, 46 *ante*] . . . In the meanwhile, Walter had become more civil, and left a note saying any article I might send should appear.

[The Diary, as well as letters to Mrs. Clarkson and to Crabb Robinson's brother, Thomas, establish the fact that Coleridge proved no more methodical in his second course of lectures than he had been in the first. The letters also show that Robinson exercised considerable tact in the details selected and emphasised for his various correspondents. Those to Mrs. Clarkson gloss over some of the lecturer's worst defects,—that to his brother (probably on this account not hitherto published) is much more plain spoken (*see* pp. 121–128.)

Crabb Robinson's impressions of these lectures are further summarised in his Reminiscences of 1849, q.v. (pp. 46, 47).

In May 1812, in the midst of all the excitement attendant on

COLERIDGE'S LECTURES

the reconciliation with Wordsworth, Coleridge was busy preparing for his third course of lectures which Crabb Robinson (who was flattered by receiving a free ticket for himself *and friends*) wrote to his brother (May 20th) were delivered at Willis's Rooms. Under date of May 9th, the Diary relates that Lady Beaumont has taken 20 tickets, but has procured no other subscribers, an omission which Coleridge " apprehends " is due to Wordsworth's presence in her house. However Wordsworth appears to have been present at the lectures on May 19th and 23rd, for Robinson notes that he " came and chatted with us a few minutes " and was introduced to members of the party. No prospectus of these lectures appears to be extant among Crabb Robinson's papers, nor are any letters preserved, with the exception of that already quoted, but the Diary is more illuminating.[1]

Thus on June 2nd. after the 4th. lecture, Godwin spoke of Coleridge " with less respect than I ever heard him before. His late lectures, he says, have convinced him that he cannot think with steadiness and effect on any one subject.

This particular course of lectures appears to have consisted of five only. They were followed in the winter of 1812–13 by a more ambitious set of twelve on " Belles Lettres," and we learn from the Diary of Nov. 3rd, 1812, the date of the first of these, that Coleridge announced to Crabb Robinson on that day that he was " about to compose lectures which are to be the produce of all his talent and power, on Education, and each lecture is to be delivered as it may be afterwards sent to the press. For this purpose he wants Spinoza." Nothing more is heard of this project : doubtless the effort to write them was sufficient to make the plan abortive. But the syllabus of the lectures on Belles Lettres at the Surrey Institute was duly issued, though it does not seem to have proved an adequate guide to their contents, wide as is the range of subjects touched upon. It is amusing to note how the summaries of the proposed discourses grow shorter and shorter as the

---

[1] [See *infra*, pp. 130–132.]

process of planning the lectures becomes irksome. Obviously Coleridge started with certain ideas of which his head was full at the time of writing, but without any clear idea whither he might be led before he reached his conclusion. Thus when he reached Lectures XI and XII, the syllabus consisted of three words, though *Milton's Paradise Lost*, might, one would have supposed, have suggested more detailed treatment. (For the prospectus of the course, and extracts from the Diary, see *infra*, pp. 132–137.)

The next, and final set of lectures in London by Coleridge were delivered in January, February and March 1818 at Fleur-de-Luce Court, Fleet St. Mr. E. H. Coleridge publishes the first draft of the prospectus in a note on p. 698 of his edition of Coleridge's Letters. The full syllabus [1] was sent to Crabb Robinson on Jan. 17, 1818, with a letter scribbled all round the margin. It is dated from Gillman's house at Highgate, by this time the poet's permanent residence.

We learn from Gillman's account that the lectures were actually written out, or at any rate delivered from notes, as Coleridge intended—an unusual proof of care and method in the preparation. However, Gillman adds that " it was obvious that his audience were more delighted when, putting his notes aside, he spoke extempore," so it may be that the poet was right when, as have many inferior speakers, he decided that for the most part a carefully thought-out plan hampered his eloquence and freedom.[2] When the mind is full of a subject, a lecturer may, and often does, speak better without detailed

[1] [Published in the 1883 volume of Coleridge's Lectures on Poetry and the Poets (Bohn). The letter has, I believe, not hitherto been printed.]

[2] [*Cf.* his own remarks on his lectures, which, he says, were the outcome of his life's thought, and not specially prepared to order, except by a few hours' thought, and by consultation of innumerable commonplace books which contained notes of his reflections upon various subjects.]

notes. But Coleridge certainly chose the path of wisdom when he determined to deliver this particular course of lectures after preparing an ordered scheme. The range of matter contemplated was excessively wide, and one less apt to digress than Coleridge might equally in this instance have been led astray. And if the syllabus was comprehensive, the objects of the course, as propounded in the prospectus, were yet more far-reaching. (See *infra*, pp. 138–143.)

Gillman, who now heard Coleridge lecture for the first time, was very greatly moved by his eloquence and brilliance, and we learn from the same admirer that this course was financially more successful than any other he had given. Crabb Robinson does not seem to have been equally impressed by the lectures though he too notes that he was gratified unexpectedly by finding a large and respectable audience, generally of very superior-looking persons.[1]

Apart from the Diary the only other reference to this course of lectures to be found in Crabb Robinson's *Remains* is contained in the following passage from a letter of Mrs. Clarkson to H. C. R. dated Nov. 25, 1818.]

". . . Do you know at all how Coleridge is going on ? I know not how it was, but I felt pleased, more than that, I felt something like a sense of obligation to Charles Lamb for noticing Coleridge in the collection of his works. It seemed like restoring a man to society who had been self-banished for a long time. You heard perhaps what an ungracious leave he took of his auditory last spring, calling them together to hear a gratuitous lecture, causing them to be told that he was too ill to meet them, but as soon as he recovered they should be sure of the lecture. Either he never recovered, or he forgot his promise. . . ."

---

[1] [See *infra*, pp. 143–145, for complete Diary references to the course.]

COLERIDGE'S LECTURES

[In the remaining sixteen years of his life Coleridge did not appear as a public lecturer, though he still continued to delight his friends with his conversational monologues. Crabb Robinson never had cause to change the opinion formed on the first day of their acquaintance, that he was " astonishingly eloquent," keeping his hearers " on the stretch of attention and admiration " whether he spoke of " politics, metaphysics, or poetry." Yet the note which sounds in the extract from Mrs. Clarkson's letter vibrates again and again in *Diary, Reminiscences* and *Letters*. Coleridge is ill or forgets his promises to fulfil engagements ; his various sins of omission and commission banish him from the society of his friends. Or, as Crabb Robinson reiterates, his splendid intellect is vitiated by want of method and concentration. Worst of all, the inward fountains of passion are dried up, afflictions bow him down to earth, until

> " each visitation
> Suspends what nature gave me at my birth
> My shaping spirit of Imagination."

—But Lamb was right. This is not the attitude for his critics to adopt, however fittingly Coleridge may himself assume it. In 1811, one of the least hopeful periods of the poet's life, Crabb Robinson was chatting with Lamb, who [1] " was serious and therefore very interesting. He corrected me, not angrily, but as if really pained by the expression ' poor Coleridge,' I accidentally made use of. ' He is a fine fellow in spite of all his faults and weaknesses. Call him Coleridge ; I hate *poor* Coleridge. I can't bear to hear pity applied to such a one.' "

The work Coleridge accomplished, the influence he diffused, the stimulus he imparted put him beyond the range of commonplace condemnation. Dr. Johnson's magnanimous summing-up of the impression left on him by Goldsmith may better represent the feeling experienced by Coleridge's friends and

---

[1] [*See* p. 43 for this passage as it appears in the *Reminiscences*.]

COLERIDGE'S LECTURES

admirers : " Let not his frailties be remembered; he was a very great man."]

I

SUMMARY OF THE LECTURE ON POETRY.
FEB. 5, 1808

" The Grecian Mythology exhibits the symbols of the powers of nature and Hero-worship blended together. Jupiter both a King of Crete and of the personified Sky.

Bacchus expressed the organic energies of the Universe which work by passion—a joy without consciousness ; while Minerva, etc. imported the pre-ordaining intellect. Bacchus expressed the physical origin of heroic character, a felicity beyond prudence.

In the devotional hymns to Bacchus the germ of the first Tragedy. Men like to imagine themselves to be the characters they treat of—hence dramatic representations. The exhibition of action separated from the devotional feeling. The Dialogue became distinct from the Chorus.

The Greek tragedies were the Biblical instruction for the people. Comedy arose from the natural sense of ridicule which expresses itself in mimicry.

Mr. Coleridge, in Italy, heard a quack in the street, who was accosted by his servant-boy smartly ; a dialogue ensued which pleased the mob ; the next day the quack, having perceived the good effect of an adjunct, hired a boy to talk with him. In this way a play might have originated.

The modern Drama, like the ancient, originated in religion. The priests exhibited the miracles and splendid scenes of religion.

Tragi-comedy arose from the necessity of amusing and instructing at the same time.

The entire ignorance of the ancient Drama occasioned the reproduction of it on the restoration of literature.

COLERIDGE'S LECTURES

Harlequin and the Clown are the legitimate descendants from the Vice and Devil of the ancient Comedy. In the early ages, very ludicrous images were mixed with the most serious ideas, not without a separate attention being paid to the solemn truths ; the people had no sense of impiety ; they enjoyed the comic scenes, and were yet edified by the instruction of the serious parts. Mr. Coleridge met with an ancient M.S. at Helmstädt, in which God was represented visiting Noah's family. The descendants of Cain did not pull off their hats to the great visitor, and received boxes of the ear for their rudeness. While the progeny of Abel answered their catechism well, the Devil prompted the bad children to repeat the Lord's Prayer backwards.

The Christian polytheism withdrew the mind from attending to the whisperings of conscience ; yet Christianity in its worst state was not separated from humanity (except where zeal for Dogmata interfered). Mahometanism is an anomalous corruption of Xtianity.

In the production of the English Drama, the popular and the learned writers by their opposite tendencies contributed to rectify each other. The learned would have reduced Tragedy to oratorial declamation, while the vulgar wanted a direct appeal to their feelings. The many feel what is beautiful, but they also deem a great deal to be beautiful which is not in fact so ; they cannot distinguish the counterfeit from the genuine. The vulgar love the Bible and also Hervey's *Meditations.*

The essence of poetry *universality.* The character of Hamlet, etc. affects all men ; addresses to personal feeling, the sympathy arising from a reference to individual sensibility spurious. (N.B. This applies to Kotzebue)."

COLERIDGE'S LECTURES

II

LETTERS FROM CRABB ROBINSON
TO MRS. CLARKSON

[The following letters[1] from Crabb Robinson to Mrs. Clarkson give a detailed and impartial account of some of the discourses which he heard :]

May 7th. 1808.

My dear Friend,

On receiving your threatning [sic] letter I inclosed it in a note to Coleridge and on calling upon him before the lecture found a letter for me very civilly written, and for which I felt grateful to you, since it was written only in the confidence he has in your judgement and was occasioned by your account of me. He has offered to give me admission constantly and I shall accept his offer whenever I can and give you a weekly letter on the subject. I shall not pretend to tell you what he says, but mention the topicks he runs over. Everything he observes on morals will be as familiar to you as all he says on criticism to me ; for he has adopted in all respects the German doctrines and it is a useful lesson to me how those doctrines are to be cloathed with *original illustrations* adapted to an English audience.

The extraordinary lecture on Education was most excellent, delivered with great animation and *extorting* praise from those whose prejudices he was mercilessly attacking and he kept his audience on the wrack [sic] of pleasure and offence two whole hours and 10 minutes and few went away during the lecture. He began by establishing a commonplace distinction neatly, between the *objects* and the *means* of education which he observed to be

---

[1] [Printed in Mrs. H. Coleridge's *Notes and Lectures on Shakespeare* (1849), and in Ashe *Coleridge's Lectures* (Bohn 1883).]

COLERIDGE'S LECTURES

" perhaps the only safe way of being useful." Omitting a *tirade* which you can very well supply on the object of E. I come to the means of forming the character, the cardinal rules of early education. These are 1. to work by love and so generate love, 2. to habituate the mind to intellectual accuracy or truth, 3. to excite power. (1) He enforced a great truth strikingly. " My experience tells me that little is taught or communicated by contest or dispute, but everything by sympathy and love. Collision elicits truth only from the hardest heads." He apologised for early prejudices with a self-correction. " And yet what nobler judgement is there than that a child should listen with faith, the principle of all good things, to his father or preceptor ?" Digressing on Rousseau, he told an Anecdote pleasantly, si non vero è ben trovato. A friend had defended the negative education of R[ousseau]. C. led him into his miserably neglected garden, choked with weeds. What is this ? said he. Only a garden, C. replied, educated according to Rousseau's principles.—On punishment he pleaded the cause of humanity eloquently. He noticed the good arising from the corporal inflictions of our great schools in the Spartan fortitude it excited, in the generous sympathy and friendship it awakened and in the point of honour it enforced : yet on the other hand he shewed this very reference to honour to be a great evil as a substitute for virtue and principle. Schoolboys, he observed, lived in civil war with their masters. They are disgraced by a lye told to their fellows ; it is an honour to impose on the common enemy : thus the mind is prepared for every falsehood and injustice when the interest of the party, when honour requires it. On disgraceful punishments such as fools-caps he spoke with great indignation and declared that even now his life is embittered by the recollection of ignominious punishments he suffered when a child ; it comes to him in disease and when his mind is dejected. This part was delivered with fervour. Could all the pedagogues of the united kingdom have been before him ! (2) On truth he was very judicious. He advised the beginning with enforcing real accuracy of assertion in young children. The parent he observed, who should hear his child call a round leaf long, would do well to fetch it instantly. Thus tutored to render words conformable with ideas, the child would have the habit of truth without having any notion of moral truth. " We should not early begin with impressing ideas of virtue, goodness, which the child could not comprehend." Then he digressed à l'Allemagne—on the distinction between obscure ideas and clear notions. Our notions resemble the index and hands of the Dial, our feelings are the hidden springs which impel the machine ; with this difference, that notions and feelings react on each other reciprocally. The veneration for the supreme being, sense of mysterious existence, not to be profaned by the intrusion of clear notions—here he was applauded by those who do not pretend to understanding, while the Socinians of course felt profound contempt for the lecturer. I find from my notes that C. was not very methodical. You will excuse my not being more so. (1 & 2.) " Stimulate the heart and mind to love and the mind to be early accurate, and all other virtues will rise of their own accord, and all vices will be thrown out." When, treating of punishment he dared to represent the text " He that spareth the rod spoileth the child " as a source of much evil—he feelingly urged the repugnance of infancy to quiet and gloom and the duty of attending to such indications. Observing that the severe notions entertained of Religion etc. were more pernicious than all that had been written by Voltaire and such " paltry *scribblers* " considering this phrase as the gilding of the pill, I let it pass. Coleridge is in the main right, but Voltaire is no paltry scribbler. A propos I could

every 20 minutes rap the knuckles of the lecturer for little
unworthy compliances for occasional conformity. But
n'importe; he says such a number of things both good and
useful at the same time that I can tolerate these drawbacks
or rather make-weights. (3.) In speaking of Education as a
means of strengthening the character he opposed our
system of " cramming " children. . . . He censured the
practice of carrying the notice [notion ?] of making learning easy, much too far, and especially satirised the good
books in Miss Edgeworth's style. " I infinitely prefer the
little books of The seven Champions of Christendom,
Jack the Giant Killer, etc. etc. for at least they make the
child forget himself, to your moral tales where a good little
boy comes in and says, Mama, I met a poor beggarman and
gave him the sixpence you gave me yesterday. Did I do
right ? O Yes my dear, to be sure you did." This is not
virtue but vanity. Such books and such lessons do not
teach goodness—but if I might venture such a word—
goodyness." What goody he referred to I know not, for
he praised Mrs. Trimmer afterwards. He afterwards
added, " The lesson to be inculcated should be, let the
Child [edge torn away] and know it not. Instructors
should be careful not to let the Intellect dye of Plethora."
     The latter part of the Lecture was taken up in a de-
fence of education for the poor—it was very useful but very
trite : he sayd nothing worth quotation. He also lugged
in most unnecessarily an attack upon Malthus—he was as
unfair in his representation as Hazlitt in his answer.
he also noticed Cobbett, etc. In conclusion he eulogised
Dr. Bell's plan of education and concluded by a severe
attack upon Lancaster for having stolen from Dr. Bell
all that is good in his plans and expatiated [with war]mth
on the barbarous ignominious punishments Lancaster introduce[d], he also accused Lancaster of religious in-
tolerance but I susp[ect, withou]t knowing the fact, that

be on this point did not do justice to the Quaker; he concluded by gratulating himself on living in this age. " For
I have seen what infinite good *one* man [can] do by
persevering in his efforts to resist evil and spread blessing
over human life. And if I were called upon to say which
two men in my own time had been most extremely useful
and who had done most for humanity, I should say Mr.
Clarkson and Dr. Bell." I cannot answer for the terms
of this sentence, the surprise I felt at the sudden introduction of your husband's name perhaps made me lose the
immediate preceding words.

I could not go on Wednesday and yesterday I went in
late. It was the least interesting lecture I have heard
tho' Milton was the subject. But the word poetry was not
used till the lecture was two-thirds over, nor Milton's name
till 10 minutes before the close. The observation or two
I may have to make I will reserve till my next letter, for,
as I said before, I mean to write weekly. I am happy
that I have thus formed Coleridge's acquaintance for tho'
we have not yet met I feel we can meet. He has given me
a general invitation for evenings. . . .

May 15th. 1808.

My dear Friend,

Be assured you have imposed on me no burthensome
task . . . I find I am a bad reporter and that I have not
the art of condensing the spirit of an hour's declamation
into a page of post paper. . . . I have only two lectures to
speak about and shall not pretend to speak of them in the
order in which Coleridge spoke since there was no order
in his speaking. I came in late one day and found him in
the midst of a deduction of the origin of the fine arts from
the necessities of our being, wh. a friend who accompanied
me could make neither head nor tail of because he had not
studied German metaphysics. The first " free art " of man

108

COLERIDGE'S LECTURES

(architecture) arose from the impulse to make his habitation beautiful, [the] 2d arose from the instinct to provide himself food, the 3d the love of dress : here Coleridge atoned for his metaphysics by his gallantry ; he declared that the passion for dress in females has been the great cause of the civilisation of mankind. " When I behold the ornaments which adorn a beautiful woman, I see the mirror of that instinct which leads man not to be content with what is necessary or useful, but impels him to be beautiful." 4. from the necessity of self-defence springs the military art and this has produced the keenest sense of honour, the finest sensibility, the character of a gentleman. 5. The ornaments of speech are Eloquence and Poetry. Here C. distinguished these arts by the characteristic that poetry is a *general* impulse ; he might have said it gives the character of what is universal to what still remains particular. Eloquence impels to particular act. Let us rise against Philip s[ai]d the Athenians when Demosthenes sat down, for D. had been eloquent. A propos, Kant observes that the Orator treats an affair of business as if it were a thing of imagination while the Poet handles a work of fancy as if it were a matter of business. Kant speaks (and Schiller expatiates on this) of the method of the 2 artists ; C. refers to the principle of the Arts, but both assertions amount to the same thing. In this same lecture Coleridge contrived to work into his speech Kant's admirably profound definition of the naïf, that it is *nature putting art to shame*. And he also digressed into a vehement but well merited declamation against those soi-disant philosophers who deny the nobler powers of man, his idealising poetic faculty and degrade him to the beast and declared he cd. not think of Buffon without horror. An assertion with which I sympathise and which is far less exceptionable than the vulgar and absurd abuse of Voltaire. But of this hereafter.

109

COLERIDGE'S LECTURES

These are metaphysics enow for the present. Now for a critical remark or two. Of Shakespeare C. observed that he alone preserved the individuality of his character without losing his own—high moral feeling is to be deduced from, tho' not in Shakesp : for the sentiment of his age was less pure than that of the preceding—not a *vicious* passage in all Shakes. tho' there are many which are gross (for grossness depends on the age). Shakes. surpasses all poets 1st. in the purity of his female characters (N.B. He declared his conviction that no part of Rich[ar]d the 3*d* except the character of Richd. was written by Shakesp. doubtless with a silent reference to the disgusting character of Lady Anne). They have no platonic refinements but are perfect wives, mothers, etc. 2*d* he is admirable for the close union of morality and passion. Shakesp. conceived that these shd. never be separated ; in this differing from the Greeks who reserved the *Chorus* for the morality. The truths he teaches he told in character and with passion. They are the " sparks from heated iron." They have all an higher worth than their insulated sententious import bespeaks. . . . A 3d characteristick is thus that Sh.'s observation was preceded by contemplation—" he first conceived what the forms of things must be and then went humbly to the oracle of nature to ask whether he was right. He enquired of her as a Sovereign, he did not gossip with her." Sh. describes feelings which no observation could teach. Sh. made himself all Characters—he left out parts of himself and supplied what might have been in himself. Nothing was given him but the Canvas (" This fact does honour to human nature for it shews that the seeds of all that is noble and good are in man—they require only to be developed ") This canvas which Shak. used formed his stories. The absurdity of his tales has often been a reproach to Sh. from those who did not comprehend him. (Johnson, Pope, etc.) but Shakesp. had nothing to do with the probability of the histories. It was enough for him that they had found their way among the people—everybody admitted them to be true, tho' childish in the extreme. There was once upon a time a king who had three daughters and he said to them, tell me how you love me and I will give my kingdom to her that loves me best; and so one daughter said etc. etc. From such stuff as this Sh. has produced the most wonderful work of human genius (as in Othello he produced the most perfect work). In the 3 first acts [sic] he carried human feelings to the utmost height, therefore in the 2 following they seem to sink and become feeble as after the bursting of the storm we behold the scattered clouds dispersed over the heavens.

Coleridge's digressions are not the worst part of his lectures or rather he is always digressing. He quoted Mrs. Barbauld under the appellation of an "amiable lady" who had asked how Richardson was inferior to Shakes. R., he allowed, evinces an exquisite perception of minute feeling but there is want of harmony and vulgarity in his sentiment. He is *only* interesting. Sh. on the other hand elevates and instructs—instead of referring to our ordinary Situations and common feelings, he emancipates us from them and when most remote from ordinary life he is most interesting. I should observe this depreciation of *the interesting* in poetry is one of the most characteristic features of the new German criticism. It is always opposed by Schiller etc. to the beautiful and is considered as a very subordinate merit indeed. Hence the severity of the attacks on Kotzebue who certainly is much more interesting to 19 out of 20 than Shakespear[e]. C. took occasion in mentioning R. to express his opinion of the *immorality* of his novels. " The higher and lower passions of our nature are kept thro' 7 or 8 volumes in a hot-bed of interest. Fielding is far less pernicious," for the gusts of laughter drive away sensuality.

III

COLERIDGE'S LECTURES

Basta ! I must bring up my arrears in my next letter but C. has begged a week's holiday as he is going to publish his lecture on education. His attack on Lancaster has given great confidence. This was to be expected. . . .

III

A.—PROSPECTUS OF THE LECTURES DELIVERED IN 1811

London Philosophical Society
Scot's Corporation Hall,
Crane Court, Fleet Street.
(entrance from Fetter Lane)

———

Mr. Coleridge
will commence
On Monday, November 18th.
A Course of Lectures on Shakespeare and Milton
in illustration of
The Principles of Poetry
and their
Applications as Grounds of Criticism to the most popular
Works of later English Poets, those of the Living included.

———

After an introductory Lecture on False Criticism, (especially in Poetry) and/on its Causes : two thirds of the remaining course will be assigned 1st. to a philosophic Analysis/and Explanation of all the principal *Characters* of our great Dramatist, as Othello, Falstaff,/Richard III, Iago, Hamlet, etc. : and 2nd., to a critical *Comparison* of Shakespeare, in respect/of Diction, Imagery, management of the Passions, Judgment in the contruction of his Dramas, in/short, of all that belongs to him as a Poet, and as a dramatic Poet, with his contemporaries, or/immediate successors, Jonson, Beaumont and Fletcher, Ford,

COLERIDGE'S LECTURES

Massinger, etc. in the/endeavour to determine what of
Shakespeare's Merits and Defects are common to him
with/other Writers of the same age, and what remain
peculiar to his own Genius./

The Course will extend to fifteen Lectures, which will
be given on Monday/and Thursday evenings successively.
The Lectures to commence at ¼ past 7 o'clock./

Single Tickets for the whole Course, 2 Guineas ;
or 3 Guineas with the privi/lege of introducing a Lady :
may be procured at J. Hatchard's, 190, Piccadilly ; J.
Murray's,/Fleet St ; J. and A. Arch's Booksellers and
Stationers, Cornhill ; Godwin's Juvenile Library,/Skin-
ner St ; W. Pople's, 67, Chancery Lane ; or by Letter
(post paid) to Mr. S. T. Coleridge,/J. J. Morgan's Esq.
No, 7, Portland Place, Hammersmith.

W. Pople, Printer, Chancery Lane, London.

B.—ACCOUNT IN DIARY OF THE 1811–1812 LECTURES

Nov. 18*th* . . Of Col.'s lecture itself I fear the genl.
opinion is not very favourable. It wanted popularity &
the moral remarks he made were not shewn to have an
immediate bearing upon the subject. I cannot myself well
judge of the effect such remarks mt. have on strangers
for to me almost every individual observation was familiar.
I had heard the same things from C. in private conversation, & frequently in a better style than in the lecture itself. There was throughout too much apology, too much
reference to what he had before written, too much promise
of what was to come. This is his great fault. In *The
Friend* he was guilty of it ; he will commit it in his
lectures. The observns. he made were in the main just &
often striking. But the lecture hardly equalled his con-

versation. Meggisson v. loudly & before the lecturer had left his rostrum, began to abuse him & alarmed me as to the general impression C. mt. have produced. . . .

Wed. 20. . . . Eveng. at Capt. Burney's ; a card-party. Col. there. I just found opportunity to intimate to him the necessy. of abstaining from apologies, prefaces &c. . .

Thursday . . . Evening at Col.'s second lecture wh. was a vast improvement on the first. It was delivered with ease, was popular & contained interesting matter on that wh. the auditors wished to hear abt. I had prepared short notes, but J. Collier having made an elaborate report wh. I can hereafter refer to, I shall reserve a connected acct. of the whole series of lectures for a future page. . . .

24th Sunday. . . . Bkfasted with Serjt. Rough & then walked with him to see Coleridge at Hammersmith. We found him not quite well but very eloquent. He soon mounted his hobby & I was not a little surprised to find him very much of a Schellingianer, of wh. I had no idea. At least his mode of comparing the fine arts & of anti- thetically considerg all their elements appeared to me very similar. He observed of poetry that it united passion with order, & he v. beautifully illustrated the nature of the human mind wh. requires & seeks to gratify contrary propensities (as sloth & the horror of vacancy) at the same time, & from this he deduced many of our likings & dis- likings. He spoke of Calderon, defining him to be a Shakespeare, but without the philosophy,—having all his imagn. & fancy. His usual distinction bet. these last mentioned qualities he repeated,—on this occasion as- signing great fancy but no imagn. to Southey, & much imagn. but a sterile fancy to Wordsw.

Our visit was short. . . .

25th Monday. . . . In the eveng. Col. delivered his 3d lecture. Excepting too much repetition in the defini- tion &c of poetry, in wh. he was not at last very successful,

& in the acct. of the Greek theatre wh. mt. have been
spared, at first he was successful till the close, when he
absurdly & almost whiningly apologised for the freedoms
he intended to use tow[ard]s certain names of authority—
Johnson, Addison &c. . . .

28. *Thursday* . . . Col.'s 4th lecture. He proceeded
to the discussion of the merits of Shakespeare & noticed
his *Venus & Adonis* on wh. he made some striking
observations, passed over to his *Tarquin & Lucrece* on
wh. he had nothg. to say, & then classified the dramas.
Finding his time not yet elapsed he again reverted
to the general topics of poetry, its essential nature &c.
& tho' some of these things were good yet the habit of thus
chewing the cud of his past lectures will be offensive.
Hearers require to have the sense of getting on & I begin
to fear that C.'s laziness will lead him to be content with
dreaming on & playing over certain favourite ideas wh.
he delights in but wh. some of his hearers will be tired of.
He certainly might with a little exertion have collected
matter enough for *one* lecture at least out of the poems
of Shakespeare. But he utterly passed over the sonnets
& made no remark on the reception the poems have met
with from modern critics.

Monday, 2nd, December . . . Col.'s 5th. lecture—an
amusing declamn. agt. Reviewers, French philosophy,
precocity etc., in the educn. of children, but unluckily
scarcely one observatn. on Shakespeare, Milton or even
on poetry. However his manner was animated and he
was apparently in good spirits.

5th Thursday. . . . Accompanied Mrs Rutt to Coleridge's lecture. In this he surpassed himself in the art
of talking very amusingly witht. speaking at all on the
subject to wh. the audience were especially invited. According to advt., C. was to lecture on *Romeo & Juliet* &
Shakespeare's female characters. Instead, he began with a

defence of school-flogging, at least in preference to Lancaster's mode of punishing, without pretending to find the least connection between that topic & poetry. Afterwards he remarked on the char[acter] of the age of Eliz. & James I, at the commencement [of] which intellect predominated, over that of Chas. I in wh. moral feeling prevailed. He distinguished between Wit & Fancy—not very clearly—; he discoursed on the character of the different languages of Europe, attacked the fashionable notion concerng poetic diction, & abused Johnson's lines " If observation with extensive view," ridiculing the tautology ; & he commented on the alleged impurity of Shakespeare & vindicated him agst the charge with warmth! The man is absolutely incorrigible but his *vitia* are indeed *splendid*. I wd. have reported for the *Morning Chronicle*, but it was too late.

While Col. was so irrelevantly commenting on Lancaster's [1] mode of punishing boys, C. Lamb whispered ' It is a pity he did not leave this till he got to *Henry vi*, & then he might say he cd. not help taking part agst. the Lancastrians.' And afterws. when Col. was so extravagantly running from topic to topic witht. any guide whatever, C.L. said : ' This is not so much amiss. C. sd. in his advt. he wd. speak abt. the Nurse in *Romeo & Juliet* & so he is delivering the lecture in the character of the Nurse. . . .

Monday 9th. . . . Tea with Rough. Accompanied Mrs. to Col's 7th & incomparably best lecture. C. declaimed with great eloquence on *Love* witht. wandering from his subject, *Romeo & Juliet*. He was spirited for the greater part, intelligible tho' profound, & he was method[ica]l.

[1] [Lancaster was a Quaker who kept a reformed school, in which novel punishments were substituted for the birch. Offenders were, *e.g.*, suspended in clothes baskets, or otherwise exposed to the ridicule of their companions. As we have seen, Coleridge strongly objected to such methods.]

Drew up a hasty report of the lecture for the *Morng. Chronicle* wh. was inserted.

10. . . . Miss Lamb dined with us. After dinner gossipped. In the eveng. C.L., Manning & Mrs. Fenwick. A pleasant eveng. C.L. spoke well abt. Shakesp. I had objected to Col.'s assertion in his lecture that Sh. became evthg. *except the vicious*, observing that if Sh. becoming a char., is to be determined by the truth & vivacity with wh. he describes them & enters into their feelings [?] C.L. justified Col.'s remark by saying (what by the bye was inclusive [conclusive ?]) that Sh. never gives truly odious & detestable chars. He always mingles strokes of nature & humanity in his pictures. I adduced the King in *Hamlet* as altogether mean. He allowed this to be the worst of Sh.'s chars. He has not another like it. I cited Lady Macbeth. ' I think this is one of Sh.'s worst characters ' sd. L.; it is at the same time inconsistent with itself. Her sleep-walking does not suit so hardened a being ' (It however occurs to me that this sleep-walking is perhaps the vindication of Sh. in his portraiture of the char. as it certainly is his excellence that he does not create monsters, but always saves the honour of human nature, if I may use such an expression. So in this. While the voluntary action & sentiments of Lady Macbeth are all inhuman, her involuntary nature rises agst. her habitual feelings, springing out of depraved passions, & in her sleep she shews to be a woman, while waking she is a monster.) I then referred to the Bastard in *Lear*, but Lamb considers his char. as vindicated by the provocn. arising out of his illegitimacy. And L. mentioned as admirable illustrations of the skill with wh. Sh. cd. make his worst chars. interesting, Iago & Richard 3. I noticed Kg. John & Lewis as if Sh. meant, like a Jacobin, to shew how base & vile kings are. L. did not remark on this, but sd. *Kg. John* is one of the plays he likes the least. He praised on the contrary *Richard* 2. . .

117

COLERIDGE'S LECTURES

Thursday 12*th.* . . . Eveng. tea with Mrs. Flaxman who accompanied me to Coleridge's lecture. C. unhappily relapsed into his desultory habit & delivered, I think, his *worst* lecture. He began with identifying religion & love, delivered a rhapsody on brotherly & sisterly love, wh. seduced him into a dissertation on incest. I at last lost all power of attending to him any longer. . . .

Sunday, 15. . . . Called on Godwin. He spoke with great severity of Col.'s lectures, wh. he thinks infinitely below his conversation in private company. That alw. impresses you with the vast extent of his knowledge. In his lectures he appears grossly ignorant G. noticed C.'s remark that Sh.'s plays are only to be read, not acted, as absolutely false. No plays but Sh.'s deserve to be represented, so well are they fitted for performance. . . .

Monday 16. . . . Afternoon a letter to brother, giving him an account of Col.'s lecture &c., and in the even., took Miss Flaxman to the lecture. C. was again very desultory during half the lecture, repeating old remarks on the analogy bet. the ancient and modern drama &c. But at length he bethought himself of Shakes : and tho' he forgot at last what we had been 4 times successively to hear, viz Romeo & Juliet as lovers, yet he began a new subject & treated beautifully of *The Tempest* & especially Prospero, Miranda, Ariel & Caliban. This part most excellent.

Thursday 19. . . . Evening at C.'s lecture, which was on *Mid. N'ts. Dream* & much less digressive than usual.

Monday 30. . . . A dinner party at Dr. Adam's. Allowed to make my retreat to Col.'s lecture . . . I had drunk too much to be quite clear-headed, however I was pleased to find C. very methodical. He kept to his subject &, in conformity with an opinion I gave him, intimated his intention to deliver 2 lectures on Milton. He had written to me stating his dilemma, having so much to do in so little time & I wrote to him an answer in wh. I gently

118

hinted at his digressions. I hope *splendida peccata* wh. his friends best apologised for by laying the emphasis on the adjective.

January 1812. *Thursday*. . . . Coleridge's lecture perhaps his very best, on *Richard* 2 & *Hamlet* &c. &c. In the latter, striking observation on the virtue of action and the futility of talents that divert from rather than lead to action. I doubt whether he did not design that an application shd. be made to himself, & whether he is not well content to meet the censure his own remarks convey for the sake of the reputation of those talents apparently depreciated.

Friday. . . . Wrote letters to Mr. Clarkson about Coleridge lectures. . . .

Thursday 9. . . . Evening Coleridge's lecture on Johnson's *Preface*. C. succeeded admirably in the exposure of Johnson & though he was sometimes obscure, the many palpable & intelligible hits must have given general satisfaction.

Monday 13. . . . Evening accompanied Mrs. C. Aiken to Coleridge's lecture. His continuation of remarks on Johnson's *Preface* very feeble & unmeaning compared with the last. He had no answer to the general faults ascribed but the complaints of the generality of the imputation. His subsequent remarks on *Lear*, a vindication of the melancholy catastrophe. On Othello, opinion that he is not a jealous character very excellent. Mrs. C. A. enjoyed the lecture. She spoke with *propriety* of C., is sensible both of his merits & demerits & has a recollection of having been neglected by him without any sense of it so strong as to take away the pleasure his lectures ought to afford.

Thursday 16. . . . In the evening at Coleridge's lecture. C. to-night began on Milton. He reviewed Johnson's *Preface* & vindicated Milton's moral & political

character with warmth, but I think with less than his
usual ability. He excited a hiss once by calling Johnson a
fellow, for wh. he happily apologised by observing that it
was in the nature of evil to beget evil & that he had therefore in censuring Johnson fallen into the same fault.
He remarked on Milton's minor poems & the nature
of blank verse & the latter half of his lecture was very
good. . . .

Monday 20. . . . Evening Coleridge's lecture ; conclusion of Milton : not one of his happiest lectures.
Among the audience Lord Byron & Rogers the banker.

Monday 27. . . . Coleridge's concluding lecture. Sat
near Mrs. Davy, but had little or no conversation with her.
She looked remarkably well & she is one of those persons
whose presence merely, delights ; her countenance &
figure alone are sufficient to spread a charm in every circle
where she is found.

The lecture was exceedingly well attended, & Coleridge
was very animated in parts. His development of the
character of Satan, his apology for Milton's mode of
treating the character of the supreme being &c. &c., were
excellent. There were some excrescences in the lecture &
he offended me by an unhandsome[1] & unmanly attack on
Mrs. Barbauld. He ridiculed some expressions in her Ode
to Content, The hamlet's brown primrose & violet &c.,—
criticisms he added, wh. Wordsworth made to me at
Charles Lamb's 2 years ago. That he shd. select among the
living authors a woman, & that woman a lady who has
been among his admirers formerly, & I believe always
shewed him civilities, is ungenerous & unworthy of his
better feelings. He analysed a passage in Pope's Homer
(a description of moonlight) & shewed its want of propriety

[1] [There is only a very slight reference to this incident in the
Reminiscences. See *ante*, p. 53. The difference is symptomatic of
the softened outlines in the later reworking of the Diary material.]

120

& taste with great spirit. At the same time he introduced
this censure with a very insincere eulogium. Mr. &
Mrs. Becker at the lecture. I joined them at Ader's :
they had been much gratified by the lecture.

Tuesday 28. . . . Wrote letters to Southey . . . [and]
to Mrs. Clarkson about Coleridge's lecture. . . .

IV

A.—LETTER FROM CRABB ROBINSON TO MRS. CLARKSON

Nov. 29th. 1811

My dear Friend,

Of course you have already heard of the lectures on
poetry which Coleridge is now delivering, & I fear have
begun to think me inattentive in not sending you some account of them, or rather I should say, of his success in the
undertaking. Yesterday he delivered the fourth, & I could
not before, form anything like an opinion of the probable
result. Indeed it is hardly otherwise now with me, but
were I to wait till I could form a judgement, the very
subject itself might escape from observation. Coleridge
has about 150 hearers on an average & I fear the number
is rather likely to diminish than encrease. A large proportion of these have been accidental droppers-in (at a dollar
a head). On the second night £12 were received at the
door ; And there may be, I should suppose about 40 who
come in with orders ; you may therefore calculate in a
great measure what the produce may be ; The ladies, I
should add, do not form above a third ; Their subscription
coming with a Gent. is only one Guinea ; he pays two
Guineas for his ticket.

A scruple just now flew in my face at having filled a
whole side with such *low* concerns, but it subsided on the

reflection that interested as I know you to be in the comfort & well-being of your friend, you will read with interest
anything that affects it materially. And certainly C.
would never have roused himself to this effort if he had not
felt an immediate want that impelled him to make it.
He has left the Courier some weeks, And I saw a letter he
had written to an old acquaintance (Serjt. Rough) in which
he frankly assigned as his inducement, the necessity of dis-
charging an old debt incurred by the publication of *The
Friend*, in order to finish the vol. in numbers & afterwards
publish quarterly volumes. This intention may perhaps be
new to you as I believe he has not yet written. He begged
me the other day to remember him most affectionately to
you ; he has been about writing to you these several
months, & he added he wanted to see me before going my
journey that I might have delivered verbal explanation
concerning his affair with Wordsworth. This was the
sole allusion he ever made to the affair ; Of course I did
not question him further. But to return to the lectures.
They have been brilliant, that is, in passages, but I doubt
much his capacity to render them popular. Or rather I
should say I doubt any man's power to render a system of
philosophy popular which supposes so much unusual attention & rare faculties of thinking in the hearer. The
majority of what are called sensible & thinking men have,
to borrow a phrase from C., " the passion of clear ideas "
& as all poets have a very opposite passion, that of warm
feelings ; & delight in musing over conceptions & imagin-
ings beyond the reach of the analytic faculty ; no wonder
there is a sort of natural hostility between these classes of
minds. This will ever be a bar to C's popularity : Besides
which he has certain unfortunate habits, which he *will* not,
(perhaps *can* not) correct, very detrimental to his interests :
I mean the vice of apologising, anticipating & repeating.
We have had 4 lectures, & are still in the prolegomena

COLERIDGE'S LECTURES

to the Shakespearian Drama ; When we are to begin
Milton I have no idea. With all these defects there will
always be a small circle who will listen with delight to his
eloquent effusions (for that is the appropriate expression).
I have not missed a lecture & have always left the room
with the satisfaction which the hearkening to the display
of truth in a beautiful form always gives. I have a German
friend who attends also & who is delighted to find the
logic & the rhetoric of his Country delivered in a foreign
language. There is no doubt that Coleridge's mind is
much more German than English. My friend has pointed
out striking analogies between C. & German authors
whom he has never seen. This is very interesting to me,
tho' I now neglect everything except the lectures for
Law. . . .

B.—LETTER FROM CRABB ROBINSON TO
MRS. CLARKSON

56 Hatton Garden
13th Dec. 1811.

My dear Friend,
   I thank you for your very acceptable letter, which I
am content to have received instead of any other you might
have written in its place. I am glad that your letter did not
arrive before mine was sent off, it would have looked as if
I needed a formal invitation to write before I could take
up the pen ; I trust that will never be the case with us.
I should have written long before had any occasion arisen
so interesting to you as Coleridge's letters ; Now I confess, I write because you fixed a period which I am unwilling to pass by ; Yesterday I should have been able to
send you a far more pleasant letter, than I can possibly
furnish you with now ; For I should then have had to
speak of one of the most gratifying & delightful exertions

COLERIDGE'S LECTURES

of C.'s mind on Monday last; & now I am both pained & provoked by as unworthy a sequel to his preceding lecture. And you know it is a law of our nature

> " As high as we have mounted in delight
> In our dejection do we sink as low."

You have so beautifully & exactly expressed the sentiment that every considerate & kind observer of your friend must entertain, that it is quite needless to give you any account of his lectures with a view to direct any judgment you might wish to form or any feeling you might be disposed to encourage ; You will I am sure anticipate the way in which he will execute his lectures.

As evidences of splendid talent, original thought & rare powers of expression & fancy, they are all his *admirers* can wish ; but as a discharge of his understanding, a fulfilment of his promise to the public, they give his *friends* great uneasiness. As you express it " an enchanter's spell seems to be upon him " which takes from him the power of treating upon the only subject his hearers are anxious he should consider, while it leaves him infinite ability to riot & run wild on a variety of moral & religious themes. In his 5th lecture he was by advertisement to speak of *Romeo & Juliet* & Shakespeare's females—unhappily some demon whispered the name of Lancaster in his ear : & we had in one Evening—an attack on the poor Quaker—a defence of boarding-school flogging—a parallel between the ages of Elizabeth & Charles—a defence of what is untruly called unpoetic language, an account of the different languages of Europe & a vindication of Shakespear[e] against the imputation of grossness ! ! !

I suspect he did discover that offence was taken at this ; for his succeeding lecture on Monday was all we could wish. He confined himself to *Romeo & Juliet* for a time, treated of the inferior characters & delivered a most

124

eloquent discourse on love with a promise to point out how
Shakespear[e] had shewn the same truths in the persons of
the Lovers. Yesterday we were to have a continuation
of the theme. Alas! C. began with a parallel between
Religion & Love, which tho' one of his favorite themes,
he did not manage successfully; He then treated of
brotherly and sisterly love, & suffered himself to be seduced
into a long digression on *incest*. Romeo & Juliet were
forgotten & in the next lecture we are really to hear something of these lovers. Now this will be the 4th time that
his hearers will have been invited expressly to hear of this
play, There are to be only fifteen lectures in the whole
(half have been delivered) & the Course is to include
Shakespear[e] & Milton, the modern poets &c ! ! ! I fear
if we look close we shall find that indolence lies at the
root of this. He *will not* look into Shakespear—the
Morgans are continually laying the book in his way; But
as if spell-bound he cannot prepare himself for his lectures;
The consequence is that he has recourse to his old M.S.
commonplace book which I daresay you well recollect;
& instead of a lecture on a definite subject; we have an
immethodical [sic] rhapsody, very delightful to you &
me, & only offensive from the certainty that it may &
ought to offend those who come with other expectations ! ! !
Yet with all this I cannot but be charmed with these
splendida vitia & my chief displeasure is occasioned by my
being forced to hear the strictures of persons infinitely below
C. without any power of refuting or contradicting them.
Yet it is lucky that he has hitherto omitted no lecture.
Living with the Morgans they force him to come with
them to the lecture room & this is a great point gained. I
only see him the Lecture Evenings now, & I fear this is
not the time to get him to write to you, but if I can judge
from his manner whenever your name is mentioned, he
would certainly read your letter; but let it not reach him

on a Thursday or Monday. In the Morning Chronicle [1]
appear after the lectures short reports "by different
hands." They serve better than an advertisement to keep
up the public attention & I have no doubt drew auditors—
I have written one, but if you do get the papers they will
furnish you with little information.

C.—LETTER FROM CRABB ROBINSON TO THOMAS ROBINSON

Dec 14. 1811.

You will I dare say be curious to know my opinion
of Coleridge's lectures. And I had thought of referring
you for that purpose to two letters written to Mrs. Clarkson ; but as I can imagine she would have no great
pleasure in reading them (your surmise in fact being well
founded) I must compress in a narrow compass & say
plainly what I wrote to her more at length & with that
management which is due to a friend. In a word then,
Coleridge's lectures do high honour to him as a man of
genius, but are discreditable to him (perhaps I might use
with[ou]t injustice a stronger word) as a man who has a duty
to discharge ; for either he wants judgement to know what
he ought to introduce in his lectures, or is overpowered by
very culpable indolence & will not qualify himself to do
justice to his subject, his hearers, or himself. His pretended
lectures are unmethodical rhapsodies, moral, metaphysical
& literary ; abounding in brilliant thoughts, fine flashes of
rhetoric, ingenious paradoxes, occasionally profound &
salutary truths but they are not a scientific or constructive
course of reading on any one subject a man can wish to fix
his attention on. He is to lecture on Shakespear[e], Milton
& the modern poets. We have in fact had one lecture on
the minor poems of Shakespear[e], & have been *three nights*

[1] [See *ante, Reminiscences,* p. 45.]

126

alone employed on *Romeo & Juliet*, which we are promised the conclusion of. The course is to consist of 15
lectures & 8 are over ! ! !

As a specimen, I will give you a syllabus of his sixth
lecture advertised to be on *Romeo & Juliet* & Shakespear's
female characters—viz : A defence of the old singing
mode of reading ; An attack upon Lancaster especially
his modes of punishment ; a defence of school-flogging.
Then by a mighty spring (tho' I could not see where he
fixed his foot to leap from) a beautiful statement of the
opposite character of the ages of Elizabeth & Ch. I.; a
commonplace dissertation on the distinct character of the
European languages ; an abuse of poetic diction à la
Wordsworth & a long attempt to vindicate Shakespeare
from the charge of impurity—However his following
lecture was most excellent : he discussed the minor
characters of *Romeo & Juliet* & delivered an eloquent
declamation on the nature of Love which he promised in
the next lecture to apply to the lovers. Alas ! the next &
last lecture was worse if possible than the sixth. He began
unhappily with an analogy he resolved to draw between
Religion & Love ; no very great undertaking for a man
of such powers of combination : But then he proceeded
to the nature of brotherly & sisterly love & gave us a
dissertation on incest. I could not attend to the rest; I
know only that we are for the 4th time to hear *Romeo &
Juliet* tonight. The fact is that C. cannot be induced to
read Shakespear[e]; and finding himself unprepared with
particular and appropriate observations : he has recourse
to his old common-place books out of which he reads
whatever chances to catch his eye. In which he certainly
finds very beautiful things which only offend me from
their being thus impertinently and irrelevantly brought
forward. By the bye if you have access to the Morning
Chronicle you will find a report of the lecture. It is

COLERIDGE'S LECTURES

written in this house; sometimes by Mr. C[ollier]
sometimes by John C[ollier] and sometimes by myself.
We are all anxious to insert the most attractive and relevant matter so that from the report you might infer more
connection than there is in fact. . . .

D.—LETTER FROM CRABB ROBINSON TO MRS. CLARKSON

56 Hatton Garden.
3 Jany 1811.
[1812, 11 by mistake]

My dear friend,

I received your letter last night & will write the
answer immediately tho' I cannot forward it till I have
seen your brother for your address. I have a better, a much
better account to give of Coleridge's lectures than formerly.
His last three lectures have for the greater part, been all
that his friends could wish, his admirers expect. Your
sister heard the two last & from her you will learn much
more than I could put into a letter had I all the leisure I
now want, or the memory I never had. His disquisitions
on the characters of Richard 3, Iago, Falstaff were full
of paradox but very ingenious & in the main true. His
remarks on Richard 2 & Hamlet very excellent. Last
night he concluded his fine development of the Prince of
Denmark by an eloquent statement of the moral of the
play. " Action " he said, " is the great end of all. No
intellect however grand is valuable if it draw us from
action & lead us to think & think till the time of action is
passed by & we can do nothing." Somebody said to me,
this is a satire on himself : No, said I, it is an elegy. A
great many of his remarks on Hamlet were capable of a
like application. I should add that he means to deliver
several lectures beyond the promised number. This will

128

gain him *credit* in the City-sense of the word & for the sake of his future success in lecturing I am very glad he is thus prudent.

You see I am viewing the subject from a very low point of view ; At the same time I am able to place myself on higher ground & then I lament equally with the Words-worths & yourself that such a man should be compelled to have recourse to such means ; But after all what is there in this lamentation more than a particular instance of the general complaint of all ages that high-mindedness should stoop to vulgarity ; that the low wants of man should drag down the elevated to low pursuits & that the noblest powers of intellect should not be accompanied with meaner but indispensable capacities. . . .

E.—LETTER FROM CRABB ROBINSON TO MRS. CLARKSON

Jan. 28. 1812

My dear Friend,

You will be interested to hear how Coleridge's lectures closed. They ended with éclat. The room was crowded, And the lecture had several passages more than brilliant ; they were luminous, And the light gave conscious pleasure to every person who knew that he could both see the glory & the objects around it at once, while, you know, mere splendour, like the patent lamps, present a flame that only puts out the eyes. C.'s explanation of the character of Satan, his vindication of Milton agt. the charge of falling below his subject where he introduces the Supreme Being, & his illustration of the difference between poetic & abstract truth & of the *diversity in identity* between the philosopher & the poet, were equally wise & beautifully demonstrated. He concluded with a few strokes of Satire ; But I cannot forgive him for selecting *alone* (Except an attack on Pope's Homer qualified by insincere eulogy)

COLERIDGE'S LECTURES

Mrs. Barbauld : She is a living writer, a woman, & a person who, however discordant from himself in character & taste, has still always shewn him civilities & attentions : She had friends in the room & the ridicule will be repeated by every one who knew the author from whom his citations were taken. It was surely ungenerous & unmanly. My only excuse for him is that he wished to fix a sting on some one & had sharpened no other. All the remarks, namely on the *brown hamlet*, the *moss rose & violet* etc. were made by Wordsworth to me while in town ; I know not who is the author of them ; they are in themselves good—but the merit of making them does not in my mind outweigh the demerit of so delivering them.—I just saw your sister at the lecture. I said I shd. write & she desired me to hint that Coleridge expressed some surprise (it might be pain) that you had not answered his letter. . . .

V

ACCOUNT IN DIARY OF THE LECTURES IN MAY AND JUNE 1812

May 19. Wordsworth called on me about 12 o'c. . . . After a cold luncheon we proceeded to Coleridge's 1st. lecture in Willis's Rooms. We heard C. about a ¼ of an hour. Of course we could not enter into it. I perceived only that he was in a digressing vein. He spoke of religion, the spirit of chivalry, the Gothic reverence for the female sex, & a classification of poetry into ancient & romantic. Mrs. Pattisson was however sufficiently delighted by the sight of eminent persons. . . . W. came & chatted with us a few moments.   . .

Saturday 23 . . . At 3 walked with Parkin to Coleridge's second lecture. P. spoke with great respect of W. but ascribed a degree of pride to him wh. he thought un-Christian & the utter absence of wh. he considered as the

peculiar excellence & glory of Xtn. heroes, viz Sir Matthew Hale. He asserts the *Eclectic Rev.* not to be unkind
nor depreciating towards W. & that his dissatisfaction with
it is a proof only of the irritableness of the poets.

Coleridge's lecture was a beautiful dissertation on the
Greek Drama. His analysis of the trilogy of Æschylus,
the Agammemnon, Orestes & Eumenides of Euripides was
interesting as well as his acct. of the Prometheus, & his
remarks on the antique tragedy, were more connected,
better & more closely than when delivered in Fetter Lane.

Tuesday 26 . . . Heard Coleridge's 3rd. Lecture. It was
wholly on the Greek drama & as he promised to proceed
this day to the modern drama, this want of progress I dare
say will do him harm with the public. His lecture was in
itself excellent & very German. He adopted the Teutonic
analogies & compared Æschylus, Sophocles, & Euripides
to Phidias, Polyclitus & Lysippus. He had imperfect conceptions & was afraid to risk entirely the Schellingian triple
classification. . . .

Friday 29*th*. . . . Coleridge's 4th. lecture. It was on
the nature of comedy, about Aristophanes &c. The mode
of treating the subject very German & of course much too
abstract for his audience, wh. was but thin. Scarcely any
ladies there. . . . At Morgan's where I spent the evening
& made a call for half an hour on Mr. [Porden ?] He had
heard Coleridge's lecture in the morning but thought him
infinitely inferior to Campbell, who, it appears is exceedingly admired. P. thinks C. makes a sad confusion of
mythology, metaphysics &c. This I have no doubt is the
general opinion, nor is it unfounded. With powers of original thought & real genius, both philosophical & poetical
such as few men in any age have possessed, Coleridge
wants certain low & minor qualities wh. render his great
powers almost inefficient & useless, while most subordinate
persons obtain all the fame he merits. . . .

COLERIDGE'S LECTURES

June 5 . . . At Coleridge's last lecture of his first course
he promised to speak of *Othello* but wasted his time on the
Winter's Tale. He digressed excessively so that he hardly
allowed himself time to point out the contrast between the
jealousy of the husband of that play & that of Othello.
In the future lectures money is to be taken at the door.
I doubt much whether the experiment will succeed. He
announced his lectures ill, as if he felt degraded by allusion
to money matters. I felt degraded at hearing a great man
refer to such a subject.

VI

A.—SYLLABUS OF LECTURES, 1812–1813

Lecture I. That to use each word in a sense peculiarly
its own is an indispensable condition of all just thinking, &
at once the surest, easiest, & even most entertaining discipline of the mind. On the words, Beautiful, Sublime,
Majestic, Grand, Picturesque, Fancy, Imagination, Taste.

Lectures II & III. The falsehood of the almost univer-
sal opinion, that, in the progress of civilised life, the in-
vention of Conveniences & Utilities precedes the Arts of
Ornament, proved by both facts, & *a priori* (i.e. from the
Nature of the Human Being). The *Fine Arts* in the
Natural Order of their Origination—Dress, Orchēsis
(including all the Arts of Bodily Motion, as Mimic
Dances, Gymnastic Sports, &c.) Architecture, Eloquence,
Music, Poetry, Statuary, Painting, Gardening.

Lecture IV. Of Poetry *in genere*, & as common to
antient Greece & to Xtendom. On the Poetry of the
Antients as contradistinguished from that of the Moderns ;
or the differences of the *Classical* from the *Romantic*
Poetry—exemplified in the Athenian Dramatic Poets.

Lecture V. On the Mythology of Antient Greece, its
Causes & Effects—& the worse than Ignorance infused by

COLERIDGE'S LECTURES

our School Pantheons—& the mistaken zeal of Religious Controversy. The connection between the Polytheism, Ethics & Republicanism of Greece : & (as thence deduced) the impossibility, & (were it possible) the uselessness of modelling our Poetry, Architecture, Music, &c. on the Remains of the Antients. The *Spirit* of Poetry common to all ages, & to *imitate* the Antients wisely, we should do as they did : that is, embody the Spirit in Forms adapted to all the Circumstances of Time, State of Society, &c.

Lecture VI. The *human* causes which the goodness of Providence directed to the Diffusion of Xtianity, & its temporal effects, abstracted from all higher & purely theological views. The Deluge of Nations—the Establishment of Xtndom—& the formation of mixed languages in wh. the decomposed Latin become amalgamated, in different proportions, with the Gothic or Celtic. These, collectively, were called the *Romance*, & in this sense of the *mixed,* as opposed to the *simple* or homogeneous, the word *Romantic* is used,—& not exclusively with reference to what we now call Romances.

Lecture VII. The characteristics of the Romantic Poetry, & the true origin of the Romantic Drama in Shakspeare. On the false points of view, from wh. Shakspeare has been regarded as wild, irregular, &c. &c. & proofs that a profound judgement in the construction of his Plays is equally his Characteristic, as Genius & deep Insight into Human Nature ;—or, rather, that they are the same power variously applied.

Lecture VIII. A philosophical Analysis of Romeo & Juliet & of Hamlet.

Lecture IX. Macbeth & Othello.

Lecture X. Hasty Review of the most important of the other Plays—& the character of Shakespeare as a Poet & as a *Dramatic* Poet.

Lectures XI & XII. Milton's Paradise Lost.

COLERIDGE'S LECTURES

B.—ACCOUNT IN DIARY OF THE LECTURES, 1812–1813

1812. *Nov.* 3. . . . At Coleridge's first lecture on Belles Lettres at the Surrey Institution. It was a repetition of former lectures & dull. He enlarged on the vagueness of terms & their abuse, & in defining taste, gave the Kantian theory as to the nature of judgments of taste. He introduced, I had almost said cantingly, some pious parenthesis about religion à la Wood, & did not on the whole gratify me exceedingly. He walked with me to A. Robinson's for Spinoza wh. I lent him. In the course of a few minutes while standing in the room, Coleridge kissed Spinoza's face at the title page, said his book was his gospel, &, in less than a minute, added that his philosophy was after all false. Spinoza's system has been demonstrated to be false, but only by that philosophy which has at the same time demonstrated the falsehood of all other philosophies. Did philosophy commence in an *It is* instead of an *I am*, Spinoza would be altogether true. And without allowing a breathing space he parenthetically asserted :—' I however believe in all the doctrines of Christianity, even of the Trinity.' A. R. afterwards observed C. has a comprehensive faith & love—but contrary to my expectation, he was pleased with these strange bursts in C. rather than offended with them—at least they seemed to impress him with a better opinion of his sincerity.

Coleridge informs me his tragedy is accepted at Drury Lane. Whitbread admires it exceedingly & Arnold, the manager, is confident of its success. C. now says he has five or six pieces ready for representation!!! At the same time he is abt. to compose lectures which are to be the produce of all his talent & power, on Education, & each lecture is to be delivered as it may be afterwards sent to the Press. For this purpose he wants Spinoza. . . .

COLERIDGE'S LECTURES

Nov. 10th. . . . . Took tea with Lamb. Then heard Coleridge's second lecture at the Surrey Institution. It was very wide of all immediate reference to polite literature. It was full of pious—cant, I fear. It treated very rhapsodically & obscurely of the primitive & barbarous state of man &c. . .

17th. . . . At Coleridge's lecture where I slept . . .

24th. . . . Eveng. heard part of a lecture by Coleridge. He was in good voice. . . .

Wednesday 25th. . . . Dined with Hamond. Coleridge, Godwin . . of the party. C. was in a tolerable mood. He was entertaining but I find after all he is a mannerist & tautologist, but his compass is greater than usual & therefore the tautology is not so soon perceived. He was rather checked by Godwin who, though he enjoys C.'s company, does not succeed in bringing him out. G. defended, but ill, Buonaparte's execution of the incendiaries at Moscow ; C. did not think it a significant enormity. I urged the tyrannous laws of Buonaparte as more odious than his immediate cruelties, & in this C. agreed. C. in the lighter parts of our conversation gave an explanation of "All my eye [&] Betsy Martin." This is a corruption of a ridicule by the Protestants at the time of the Reformation of the Catholic address on the feast of St. Martin. Mihi beate Martini !! Si non vero è ben trovato. . . .

1812. *Tuesday, December* 1. . . . Evening at Coleridge's lecture, Surrey Institution. Three-fourths of the lecture a declamation on Atheism. He meant to introduce by a reference to religion, the German antithesis between paganism & Christianity, which was itself to be merely an introduction to the contrast between classic & romantic poetry. But as usual he wasted his time on the introduction to the introduction ! . . .

6. . . . At Morgan's found Coleridge in good spirits. He is now about to devote himself to the Drama & wants

135

Goethe's works for the sake of availing himself of his songs in his operas.

8th. . . . . In the evening I was at a lecture from Coleridge in which was not even a single word on the subject of polite literature in any way. Though he began with an apology for talking too much about atheism last Tuesday, in this lecture he spoke of nothing but Italy & the circumstances of its early history.

1813. Tuesday [Jan] 5th. In the eveng. at Coleridge's lecture. Heard but a little.

Tuesday 12th. In the eveng. at Coleridge's lecture.

19th. At Coleridge's lecture. Very eloquent & popular on the genl. char. of Shakespeare : he is recoverg. lost character among the Saints . . .

Saturday 23rd. . . . Eveng. at Drury Lane, the first performance of Coleridge's Tragedy Remorse. Sat with Amyot, The Hamonds, Godwins &c. My interest for the play was greater than in the play. And my anxiety for its success took from me the feeling as a mere spectator I shd. have had. I have no hesitation however in sayg. that its poetical is far greater than its dramatic merit ; that it owes its success rather to its faults than its beauties, & that it will have for its less meritorious qualities applause wh. is really due for its excellencies. (Mem : it was subsequently acted [? Blank in MS.] nights during the season.) C.'s great fault is that he indulges before the public in those metaphysical & philosophical speculations wh. are becoming only in solitude & with select minds. His two great characters are philosophers of C.'s own school, the one a sentimental moralist, the other a sophisticated villain : both are dreamers. In [sic] two experiments made by Alvez on his return, the one on his mistress by relating a dream, & the other when he tries to kindle remorse in the breast of Ordonzo, are too subtle & fine-spun to be intelligible. So when Ordonzo enigmatically reproaches Isidore with his

136

guilt, he tries the cunning of the audience to find out his drift. However in spight of these faults, of the improbability of the action, of the clumsy contrivance with the picture & the too ornate & poetic diction throughout, the tragedy was recd. with great & almost unmixed applause & was announced for repetition without any opposition.

26. In the eveng. heard Coleridge's concluding lecture at the Surrey Institution. He was received with three rounds of applause on entering the lecture room & very loudly applauded at the close. During the eveng. he gained great applause by some eloquent moral reflections. And he this eveng. as well as on the 3 or 4 preceding nights redeemed the reputation he lost at the commencemt of the course. That Coleridge shd. ever become a popular man wd. once have been thought a very idle speculation. It depends on himself & if he wd. make a sacrifice of some peculiar[itie]s of taste (His enemies assert he has made many on essential points of religion & politics) he has talents enough to command success, but he must also add the power of repressing the avowal of his own favourite peculiarities in opinion & feeling which I doubt he will never be able to obtain. His general notions on party topics will suit a large proportion of the public, & though he is not yet a favourite, there is a general opinion in favour of his genius.

VII. 1818 LECTURES

A.—LETTER FROM COLERIDGE TO CRABB ROBINSON [1]

My dear Sir,

Let me entreat your kind offices, as far as your influence extends, in favor of your old Lecturer. Were any spur wanting but your own friendliness, I could state claims

[1] [This letter is scribbled in the margins of the prospectus which is printed overleaf (B).]

COLERIDGE'S LECTURES

eno' on the support of the Friends of Literature & Philosophy. But Charles or Mary Lamb can inform you of the
infamous manner in which I have been swindled by the
Reverend Curtis & his accomplices.[1] If you think you
could scatter a few Prospectuses advantageously for me,
you may have any number at Charles Lamb's (where by
the bye I left your umbrella) any time after Monday
afternoon. I shall have written every lecture first as if I
[intended to read them ?] but shall deliver them without
book which plan will, I trust, answer all purposes, that of
order in the matter & of animation in the manner. I
honestly confess to you that I feel my heart broken :
& am convinced that I shall not have many favors to ask
of my friends. If I depart however, "an entire man,"
with my intellectual faculties unclouded & with my
Moral Being uncankered by Envy, Malice & Hatred—
tho' killed yet not conquered by the world, & undebased
by the selfishness that grasps—which gripes & holds fast,
or that which shrinks back or skulks off, I shall not regret
that I have lived to subscribe myself as I again do most
sincerely, yours faithfully &with high regard [and] esteem,
S. T. Coleridge.

P.S. When will you come & dine with us ? On the
Sunday after next, should the day be fine, I am in hopes
that Charles & his sister will come up. Can you meet them ?

B.—PROSPECTUS AND SYLLABUS
of
A COURSE OF LECTURES
by S. T. COLERIDGE.

There are few families, at present, in the higher &
middle classes of English society, in which literary topics
& the productions of the Fine Arts, in some one or other

[1] [I am unable to explain this sentence.]

138

of their various forms, do not occasionally take their turn in contributing to the entertainment of the social board, & the amusement of the circle at the fireside. The acquisitions & attainments of the intellect ought, indeed, to hold a very inferior rank in our estimation, opposed to moral worth, or even to professional & specific skill, prudence & industry. But why should they be *opposed*, when they may be made subservient merely by being *subordinated?* It can rarely happen that a man of social disposition, altogether a stranger to subjects of taste (almost the only ones on which persons of both sexes can converse with a common interest), should pass through the world without at times feeling dissatisfied with himself. The best proof of this is to be found in the marked anxiety which men who have succeeded in life without the aid of these accomplishments shew in securing them to their children. A young man of ingenuous mind will not wilfully deprive himself of any species of respect. He will wish to feel himself on a level with the average of the society in which he lives, though he may be ambitious of *distinguishing* himself only in his own immediate pursuit or occupation.

Under this conviction, the following Course of Lectures was planned. The several titles will best explain the particular subjects & purposes of each ; but the main objects proposed, as the result of all, are the two following :

I. To convey, in a form best fitted to render them impressive at the time, & remembered afterwards, rules & principles of sound judgment, with a kind & degree of connected information, such as the hearers, generally speaking, cannot be supposed likely to form, collect, & arrange for themselves, by their own unassisted studies. It might be presumption to say, that any important part of these Lectures could not be derived from books ; but none, I trust, in supposing, that the same information

139

could not be so surely or conveniently acquired from such
books as are of commonest occurrence, or with that
quantity of time & attention which can be reasonably expected, or even wisely desired, of men engaged in business
& the active duties of the world.

Under a strong impression that little of real value is derived by persons in general from a wide & various reading ;
but still more deeply convinced as to the actual *mischief* of
unconnected & promiscuous reading, & that it is sure,
in a greater or less degree, to enervate even where it does
not likewise inflate ; I hope to satisfy many an ingenuous
mind, seriously interested in its own development &
cultivation, how moderate a number of volumes, if only
they be judiciously chosen, will suffice for the attainment
of every wise & desirable purpose : that is, *in addition* to
those which he studies for specific & professional purposes. It is saying less than the truth to affirm, that an
excellent book (& the remark holds almost equally true of
a Raphael as of a Milton) is like a well-chosen & well-
tended fruit-tree. Its fruits are not of one season only.
With the due & natural intervals, we may recur to it year
after year, & it will supply the same nourishment & the
same gratification, if only we ourselves return with the
same healthful appetite.

The subjects of the Lectures are indeed very *different*,
but not (in the strict sense of the term) *diverse :* they are
various, rather than miscellaneous. There is this bond of
connexion common to them all,—that the mental pleasure
which they are calculated to excite is not dependent on
accidents of fashion, place, or age, or the events or customs
of the day ; but commensurate with the good sense, taste,
& feeling, to the cultivation of which they themselves so
largely contribute, as being all in *kind*, though not all in
the same *degree*, productions of *Genius*.

What it would be arrogant to promise, I may yet be

COLERIDGE'S LECTURES

permitted to hope,—that the execution will prove correspondent & adequate to the plan. Assuredly, my best
efforts have not been wanting so to select & prepare the
materials, that, at the conclusion of the Lectures an attentive auditor, who should consent to aid his future recollection by a few notes taken either during each Lecture
or soon after, would rarely find himself, for the time to
come, excluded from taking an intelligent interest in any
general conversation likely to occur in mixed society.

S. T. Coleridge.

SYLLABUS OF THE COURSE

Lecture I. Tuesday Evening, January 27, 1818.—On
the Manners, Morals, Literature, Philosophy, Religion, &
the State of Society in general, in European Xtdom, from
the 8th. to the 15th. Century (that is, from A.D. 700 to
A.D. 1400), more particularly in reference to England,
France, Italy, & Germany : in other words, a portrait of
the (so-called) Dark Ages of Europe.

Lecture II. Friday Evening, Jany. 30.—On the Tales
& Metrical Romances common, for the most part, to
England, Germany, & the North of France ; & on the
English Songs & Ballads, continued to the Reign of
Charles the First.—A few Selections will be made from
the Swedish, Danish, & German Languages, translated
for the purpose by the Lecturer.

Lecture III. Tuesday Evening, Feby. 3.—Chaucer &
Spenser ; of Petrarch ; of Ariosto, Pulci, & Boiardo.

Lectures IV, V, VI, on *Friday Evening*, Feb. 6 ; on
Tuesday Evening, Feb. 10 ; & on *Friday Evening, Feby.*
13.—On the Dramatic Works of Shakespeare. In these
lectures will be comprised the substance of Mr. Coleridge's
former Courses on the same subjects, enlarged & varied by
subsequent study & reflection.

141

COLERIDGE'S LECTURES

Lecture VII. Tuesday Evening, Feby. 17.—On Ben Jonson, Beaumont & Fletcher, & Massinger ; with the probable Causes of the Cessation of Dramatic *Poetry* in England with Shirley & Otway, soon after the Restoration of Charles the Second.

Lecture VIII. Friday Evening, Feby. 20.—Of the Life & *all* the Works of Cervantes, but chiefly of his Don Quixote. The Ridicule of Knight-Errantry shewn to have been but a secondary Object in the Mind of the Author, & not the principal Cause of the Delight wh. the Work continues to give in all Nations, & under all the Revolutions of Manners & Opinions.

Lecture IX. Tuesday Evening, Feby. 24.—On Rabelais, Swift & Sterne : on the Nature & Constituents of genuine Humour, & on the Distinctions of the Humourous from the Witty, the Fanciful, the Droll, the Odd, etc.

Lecture X. Fri. Eveng. Feby. 27. Of Donne, Dante & Milton.

Lecture XI. Tuesy. Eveng. March 3. On the Arabian Nights Entertainments, & on the *romantic* Use of the Supernatural in Poetry, & in Works of Fiction not poetical. On the Conditions & Regulations under which such Books may be employed advantageously in the earlier Periods of Education.

Lecture XII. Friday Eveng., March 6.—On Tales of Witches, Apparitions, &c. as distinguished from the Magic & Magicians of Asiatic Origin. The probable Sources of the former, & of the Belief in them in certain Ages & Classes of Men. Criteria by which mistaken & exaggerated Facts may be distinguished from absolute Falsehood & Imposture. Lastly, the Causes of the Terror & Interest which Stories of Ghosts & Witches inspire, in early Life at least, whether believed or not.

Lecture XIII. Tuesday Eveng., March 10.—On Colour, Sound, & Form, in Nature, as connected with

COLERIDGE'S LECTURES

Poesy : the word " Poesy " used as the *generic* or class term, including Poetry, Music, Painting, Statuary, & ideal Architecture, as its Species. The reciprocal Relations of Poetry & Philosophy to each other ; & of both to Religion, & the Moral Sense.

Lecture XIV. Friday Evening, March 13.—On the Corruptions of the English Language since the Reign of Queen Anne, in our Style of writing Prose. A few easy Rules for the Attainment of a manly, unaffected & pure Language, in our genuine Mother Tongue, whether for the purposes of Writing, Oratory, or Conversation. Concluding Address.

By permission of the Philosophical Society of London, the Lectures will be delivered at their Great Room, Fleur-de-Luce Court, Fleet St., & will commence on each Evening at a Quarter after Eight precisely.

Single Subscription Tickets for the whole Course, *Two Guineas each :* & Tickets admitting a Gentleman & Lady, *Three Guineas each :* may be procured at Messrs. Taylor & Hessey, 93, Fleet Street ; Hookham & Sons, Old Bond-Street; Boosey & Sons, New Broad-St; & at the Society's Rooms, on the Lecture Nights.

Admission to the single Lecture, *Five Shillings.*

Jas. Adlard & Sons, Printers, 23, Bartholomew Close.

C.—ACCOUNT IN THE DIARY OF THE LECTURES, 1818

[Attendance curtailed by Circuit]

Jan. 27. 1818. . . . Taking Mrs. Collier with me, I went to a lecture by Coleridge in Fleur de Luce Court, Fleet St. I was gratified unexpectedly by finding a large & respectable audience—generally of very superior looking persons—in physiognomy rather than dress. But the lecture was heavy. C. treated of the origin of poetry & of Oriental work, but he was little animated & an exceedingly bad cold rendered his voice scarcely audible.

Jan. 30th. . . . I then went to Coleridge's second lecture. It was much more brilliant than the first & seemed to give general satisfaction. . . .

Feb. 3d. . . .I accompanied Mrs. Collier to Coleridge's lecture. C. lectured on Dante, Ariosto etc.—more entertainment than instruction—splendid irregularities throughout.

Feb. 6th. . . After 8 I accompanied Mrs. John Collier to Coleridge's Lecture which was like his other lectures in most particulars but rather less interesting. He treated of Shakespear & dwelt on mere accidents which served to bring out some of his favourite ideas which, after a certain number of repetitions become tiresome.

Feb. 10th. . . . I was obliged to leave the party [at Walter's] to attend Coleridge's lecture—On Shakespear and as usual ; but he was apparently ill—I went alone, neither Miss Flaxman nor Mrs. Collier could go.

Feb. 12th. . . . I called late on Lamb who does not attend Coleridge's lectures. C. has not sent him a ticket which I cannot account for.

Feb. 13th. . . . Coleridge's lecture to which I accompanied Mrs. Flaxman. I left Flaxman very poorly. The lecture was as usual, interesting.

Feb. 17th. . . . I then went alone to Coleridge's lecture. He spoke of Ben Jonson, Beaumont & Fletcher &c. —spoke of their impurity etc. as he had done before & further convinced me that his circle of favourite ideas, he is confined within as much as any man—& that his speculations have ceased to be living thoughts, in which he is making progress. They are closed, I believe, & he has not the faculty of giving them consistency & effect.

COLERIDGE'S LECTURES

Feb. 20th. . . . We found the lecture-room fuller than I had ever seen it & were forced to take back seats, but it was a pleasure to Mrs. Pattisson to sit behind Sir James Mackintosh. He was with Serjeant Bosanquet & Rolland & some genteel woman. The party was however in a satirical mood & made sneering remarks as it seemed, throughout the lecture. Indeed Coleridge was not in one of his happiest moods to-night. His subject was Cervantes but he was more than usually prosing & his tone peculiarly drawling. His digressions on the nature of insanity were carried too far & his remarks on the book but old & by him often repeated.

Feb. 24th. . . . The lecture was on Wit & Humour & the great writers of wit & humour. There was much obscurity & metaphysics in the long introduction & not a little cant & commonplace in the short criticisms. I fear that Coleridge will not on the whole add to his reputation by these lectures.

Feb. 27th. . . . Coleridge's lecture. It was on Dante & Milton—one of his very best. He digressed less than usually & really gave information & ideas about the poets he professed to criticise.

THE ESTRANGEMENT BETWEEN
COLERIDGE & WORDSWORTH

A.—EXTRACTS FROM THE DIARY

1811. *Sunday, July* 21. . . . A call on Serjt. Rough, Housmann & C. Lamb. L. had met with an accident. (H. Wedd had nearly put out his eye by throwing a pen full of ink into it.) He intimated that Wordsw. had lately treated Coleridge with great unkindness & made him quite wretched. He had warned Montagu not to take him into his house. This had afflicted C. & W. had not taken any notice of it, tho' he knew how much he had been affected by the circumstance . . .

1812. Sunday, May 3. C. spoke to me for the first time about Wordsworth's quarrel with him & with permission for me to repeat to W. all he said. Coleridge made no objection whatever to see W. either alone or in the presence of friends, but he will not consent to the proposal made that he shd. meet W. with Montagu in order that he & M. shd. be confronted. ' I cannot endure to meet a man like M. & to stand a trial with him wh. of us is a liar. I will write to W. [in] detail of all M. said to me. I will confirm it with the most solemn of oaths.—I will believe implicitly anything W. says.' This was called forth by my observing (under the impression that C. refused to meet W.) that after the intimacy so long maintained bet. C. & W. each shd. give to the other entire faith & not listen to any third person agst. the other. C. was ready to assent to this principle. A proposal has been made that Josiah Wedgwood shd. be a sort of arbitrator, but C. justly observed ' Of all men Wedgwood is the most unfit. He is my *benefactor*, he has made me independent. However I can submit to such an exam[inatio]n by no one. Morgan & the ladies are quite indignant at the very thoughts of it. C.

146

then added very strong intimations of his disesteem for
Montagu ; said, if he were pressed, he shd. be obliged to
state how grossly M. has calumniated Wordsworth. ' But
this,' said C., ' wd. force me to involve other persons [of] a
most respectable family. Besides, to what purpose shd. two
meet to call each other liar ? And if we both persist in
what we assert, we must end the dispute as men of honour
are in the habit of doing : we must fight.' C. also said :
' One of these three things might be true ; a fourth is not
possible. Either W. has treated me most unkindly & in a
manner in wh. no friend ought to have done, or I am a
most ungrateful & vile wretch (the words were more
emphatic than these) or M. is a liar.' The result of all was
a reiteration of his willingness to see W. ; his determination
not to see M. I shd. add that throughout he spoke with
strong feeling of reverence for W. ' I complain of W.'s
conduct towards me. I have nothing to say agst *him*. I
should not have been almost killed by this affair, if it had
not been that I had loved W. as a great & good man. I
wd. have sacrificed even my external reputation for him.
And I shd. not have felt as I have done, if I had not felt
that I must love W. less than before.' C. then burst into
strong exclamations. ' What friend have I ever lost !
Who that ever did love me has ever ceased to love me ? '
I did not feel it safe to ask C. why he refused to call on W.
when in the North—partly because in an affair like this
I do not like to ask a question wh. looks like intrusion,
partly from an ignorance of the real facts & partly from a
reluctance to put a question wh. I fear cannot be answered
by the person to whom I am addressing myself.

    *   *   *   *   *

   C. said, (to revert to our conversation) that he knew he
had resolved *not* to stay at M.'s house, & this remark
seemed to confirm the original report, viz. that M. excused himself to C. for C. said that M. did actually make

use of the phrase. ' C. has rotted his entrails out with ' &c &c. I did not mention Mrs. Clarkson's name. . . .

1812. *Fri. May* 8. I delivered Coleridge's message to W. & this led to a long conversation & to a commission wh. W. gave me, viz. in answer to C.'s message to say to him the following :—

(1) That he, W. denied most positively having ever given to Montagu any commission whatever to say anything as from him W. to C.; that he said nothing to M. with any other than a friendly purpose towards both C. & M. ; that he was anxious to prevent C.'s going into M.'s family because he knew that such an intimacy wd. be broken as soon as it was formed, & lead to very painful consequences. Under this impression only he spoke with M. But he takes blame to himself for being so intent upon attaining this object as to forget that M. was not a man whose discretion could be safely trusted with even so much as he did say to him.

(2) He denies having ever used such a phrase as *rotten drunkard ;* such an expression he could not, as a man of taste merely, have made use of.

(3) Neither did he ever say that C. *had been a nuisance in his family.* He might in the course of conversation & in reference to certain particular habits have used the word nuisance, wh. is a word he frequently makes use of, but he never employed it as the result or summary of his feelings towards C. He never said *he* was a nuisance.

(4) Further he wished to inform C. that he no longer wished to confront him & M. He was content to leave undetermined who had erred, but he expected from C. that when he, W. had made this declaration, he C. wd. give him credit for the truth of it & not continue to use that language about him wh. he had done.

These points I distinguish from the rest of W.'s statement because they are those I did afterwards repeat to C., except perhaps the conclusion of the last wh. I might not distinctly state to C.

W. added other remarks wh. I was careful not to repeat as they could not tend to the reconciliation so desirable & perhaps so important to the future happiness of C. W. did not deny having said he had no hopes of C. & with respect to the phrase ' rotting out his entrails by intemperance,' he does not think he used such an expression, but the idea might be conveyed in what he said & M. might give that as the conclusion from all he said. W. also denied & indignantly, that he ever meant to drive away C. by indirectly inform-ing him through M. of what he did not choose to com-municate directly himself. This I also stated to C. W. did not deny having said, 'I have no hopes of him.' 'I have long had no hopes of him, but I wd. not say so to C. be-cause I wd. not act as if I had hopes. Besides he has lately done more than I expected & exerted himself beyond my hopes.' On my observing to him that C. possibly might require that W. shd. make his election between him & M., W. replied he could not do this ; he had never acted on this principle, & had he done so, he shd. have quarrelled with every friend he has, but, added he, ' if M. should assert that I said those things wh. I now deny, then I will never speak to him again.' Excepting the last line, W. ob-served that C. had probably been so much pained by being forced to contemplate certain truths respecting himself, that in refuge he sought to load him, W. with the blame. C.'s habits had in fact been of a kind wh. he, W., could not have endured but for the high estimation he had formed of C. W. with no faint praise, then spoke of C.'s mind, the powers of which he declared to be greater than those of any man he ever knew. From such a man, under favour-able influences, everythg. might be looked for. His genius he thought to be great but his talents still greater, & it is in the union of so much genius with so much talent that C.

surpasses all the men W. ever knew. In a digression to wh. this remark led, W. observed of himself that he, on the contrary, has comparatively but little talent ; genius is his characteristic quality.

If genius (in this relation) be creation & original production from the stores of individual mind, & talent shew itself in the power of appropriating & assimilating to itself the product of foreign minds, & by so imbibing & adding to its own possessions the attainments of other minds, then I have always given to W. & C. the respective superiority in genius & talents. W. also wished to inform C. that he had not opened his letter because it was written *before* he had sent to C. that he wished to receive from him a dry statement of the assertions of M. & he wished to be spared all other subjects. (This I did repeat & I stated also to C. that W.'s manner was not *insulting* or unfriendly when he said this, for I found that C. had so interpreted W.'s former message & note to C.L. to this effect.) W. also intimated no objection to see C. but would rather not see him alone. He was fearful of those bursts of passion or rather weakness of wh. C. is capable. On one occasion, he stated, that in a large company, Sir Henry Englefield attacked him, C. in a gross way on his lecture at the Royal Institution against Lancaster. C., instead of defending himself, burst into tears. (This led W. to observe on the false sensibility & tendency to tears in the present age. What, said he, would our glorious ancestors have thought of a First Lord of the Admiralty who cries in the House of Commons when he speaks of the lives lost on a shipwreck, or of an Attorney-General who, when prosecuting men for high treason—the soldiers taken in the East Indies—is so affected that he cannot proceed.)

These are a few only of the many things said to me by W. I walked with him to Newman St. & proceeded immediately to C. What I said to him is already stated in the

preceding account of my conversation with W. C. mani-
fested certainly more feeling than W. He was greatly
agitated & affected, even to tears. He promised to draw
up the brief statement W. requested & I am to have this
on Sunday morning. But C. received W.'s declarations
with less satisfaction than I could have wished. He said
' Had W. *at first* denied using the language employed by
M., had he stated ' I said what I did say purely out of
friendship & I regret having said so much to a man like
M.' the only affair wd. have been as a cobweb between W.
& my love of him.'

C. then burst into strong expressions of his love for W.
He asseverated with great earnestness that M. expressly
said : ' Mr C. I have it in commission from Mr. W. to say
to you ' & then proceeded in his impassioned way to state
how he was affected by these assertions & circumstances of
confirmation, such as Mrs. M. saying ' I thought it not
friendly in Mr. W.' to go into such detail (or dwell on such
a subject). And she also said : ' I thought the facts stated
by W. did not warrant his conclusions.' C. evidently believed M., notwithstanding his own bad opinion of his
veracity. This I intimated to C. & this he justified. As to
the phrase ' rotted his entrails out &c,' ' I could not
forget,' said C., ' that W. had on leaving me reminded [me]
of the fact *you* stated concerning Schiller, that when he was
opened his entrails were, as it were, eaten up while his
brain was sound. And W. used the very same expressions
speaking of Schiller wh. M. did.' This circumstance abt.
S. W. had mentioned to me. He reminded C. of it in
answer to C.'s remark that he felt his head not weak.
C. further complained of W.'s taking part with M., going
at once to his house &c. &c. I observed to C. on this that
his not calling at W.'s when lately in the Lakes sufficiently
justified W. in not seeking him. C. did not satisfactorily
answer me on this head. He referred to W.'s cold answer

to a letter written by Miss Lamb. (I shd. have stated before that W. dwelt on this circumstance with more warmth than any other, particularly on the injustice done to his sister, who had been C.'s best friend at all times.) And he seemed to be impressed with the idea of W.'s not having felt towards him as his friend. I endeavoured to draw C.'s attention from *words* wh. are so liable to misrepresentation, & wh. in repetition so entirely change their character, to the fact so positively denied by W., that he never intended, least of all commissioned M. to repeat what W. stated to him. This in my mind is the only material fact. Everythg. else admits of explanation : this does not. C. asserted further that from his manner he inferred that W. meant that C. shd. conclude that from what he had said to M. that he did not wish C. to be again under his roof. This inference I strenuously denied. My conversation with C. did not last long. I was apprehensive of saying too much. C. seemed less inclined than usual to say much. I offered that the statement by C., if he had a difficulty in addressing it to W., might be to me or to no one.

Wrote a note to W. making an appointment for Sunday. . . .

Saturday 9th. A call on C. Lamb. Found Miss Lamb with him, to my great satisfaction. I chatted a short time. He is of opinion that any attempt to bring W. & C. together must prove ineffectual. Perhaps he thinks it mischievous. He thinks W. cold. It may be so : healthful coolness is preferable to the heat of disease. He thinks W.'s arrival at London a most unhappy thing for C. who apprehends his presence at Sir G. Beaumont's will operate to his disadvantage. Lady B. has taken 20 tickets but she has procured no other subscribers. C. is certainly disturbed by W.'s being in town & the effect upon his lectures may be bad.—Borrowed of L. his *Mr. H.* which, in the evening, I read at Mrs. Barbauld's to Mrs. & Miss Aiken, Mrs. &

COLERIDGE AND WORDSWORTH

Miss Kinder. They all appeared to enjoy it very much.
The sincerity with wh. they praised L. & his pieces does
the family credit. My visit was spent in this reading & in a
game of chess. . . . The Aikens, though not sensible of
the exclusive worth of W.'s poetry, still speak with respect
of him. Neither he, however, nor his friends can or ought
to receive a praise that is given him in common only with
all sorts of pretended poets. Mrs. B. prefers to all others
the Idyll—the return of a brother who finds his brother &
friends all dead. [*The Brothers.*]

Sunday 10*th.* Called by appointment on Coleridge. I
found him writing the promised statement wh. he read to
me but was too much affected to be able to proceed. The
statement contained the most indubitable internal evidence
of truth. The facts are nearly those anticipated in W.'s
denial on Friday & the paper, tho' not elaborately drawn
up or artfully written, produced the due effect on W.'s
mind, to whom I carried it immediately, & with whom I
spent the remainder of the morning. W.'s conversation was
very interesting. Much was confidential, & in writing
abt. it, I will not forget that what I ought to *say* to no one,
I ought still less to *write* what anybody by possibility may
say [sic]. I hope in these Memoranda I have never violated this principle & that I have recorded nothing wh. a
friend could ever reproach me with as an indiscretion. A
great part of W.'s conversation both to-day & to-morrow
[sic] was of a kind not to be repeated. As what I may relate,
however, will come with propriety under Monday's date,
I will bring all under that head. After a long conversation
on C., W. & I walked towards the City, & called on Serjt.
Rough & the Colliers. . . .

11*th.* At ½ past 10 with W. by appointment & left him
in Oxford Rd. past two. The morning was spent in answering C.'s statement, wh. W. had great difficulty to do because he had to reconcile things very difficult to unite—

153

the most exact truth & sincerity with the giving his friend
the least possible pain. The objections therefore that were
made to particular expressions that might be liable to one
of two objections were innumerable. The purport of the
letter was a denial most direct & comprehensive that he
had given to M. any commission whatever to say to C.
anythg. whatever, & a denial, as to the particular words
alleged, that any of them were used in the spirit imputed to
them ; an assertion that all he said was to prevent an
intimacy between M. & C. with no thought that it could
affect his own intimacy with C.; & a confession that he
was to blame in saying so much to a man so indiscreet as
M.: an expression of his belief in C.'s sincerity in making
the statement & at the same time of his wish not to enquire
whether he misunderstood M. or M. misunderstood him,
W., or how the misapprehension originated, W. declaring
that the love & affection he bears to C. & that C. he trusts,
bears to him, not needing [do not need] a solution of these
difficulties. But shd. C. still entertain doubts, then he,
W., would require to have his declarations confirmed by
M. tho' this must lead to an opening of the differences bet.
C. & M. This was the effect of the letter. The conversation that accompanied the writing it, was highly interesting
& exhibited W. in a most honourable light. His integrity,
his purity, his delicacy are alike eminent. How preferable
is the *coolness* of such a man to the heat of C. The *opinion
entertained by W. of Montagu and his wife* greatly
facilitated the writing a conciliatory letter. *W. I find
believed the latter [*i.e.* Coleridge] fully.* [1]

I was greatly edified by the manner in wh. W. incidentally treated a subject wh. has often perplexed me. I have
frequently thought it a subject of reproach in Godwin [2] &
others to associate with persons for whom they entertain

[1] [The words between asterisks are in shorthand in the original.]
[2] [Original word in shorthand.]

no esteem. And yet there is an attention due to those whom we may not admit into the penetralia of our hearts, wh. kindness may inspire & humanity sanction. The difficulty lies in the liability to err by manifesting an appearance of esteem not really felt, & a truly benevolent man like W. will be exposed to misconception, since what in him is a generous, merely generous sensibility to the happiness of others will have the warmth of personal & exclusively personal attachment in common people. W. spoke eloquently of the difficulty of breaking off an intimacy early formed, more especially where a benefit is conferred by that intimacy & where, by the influence of friendship, characters are preserved from lapses that might otherwise prove their shipwreck. These remarks had no reference to W.'s feelings towards C. for whom he expressed an admiration quite enthusiastic & whose goodness of heart too he praised. He made observations, it is true, wh. would have pained C. to hear, but these were dictated by necessity & were never made in any other than an affectionate spirit.[1] But of Montagu W. spoke in a very different manner. I ought not to put in writing what he said. W. wished not to have the points of C.'s letter discussed because if Montagu persisted in making such statements as C.'s letter contained W. must cease all further acquaintance with him. Of Mrs. Montagu he also expressed a decidedly bad opinion. But she is the wife of my friend, sd. W. W. has known Montagu many years & has been of the most essential service to him &c. &c. but of his veracity he has a very bad opinion indeed : of Coleridge his opinion is not good, though on this occasion his letter bore indubitable marks of sincerity about it. I shd. add that the great part of the letter was written by me. W. being by no means tenacious of what he had written [word erased],

[1] [From here to the end of the paragraph is a mixture of short and longhand in the original.]

willing to say anything he could truly, to give C. satisfaction.

Dr. Wordsworth joined us & we walked into Oxford St. together. Coleridge was not at home. After an early dinner . . . I went again to C. where I found the Lambs. I had just heard of what had taken place about an hour & a half before,—the assassination of Mr. Percival. This news shocked C. exceedingly. He spoke with great warmth of esteem for Percival, much more indeed than I think in any way merited by P. C. was at once ready to connect this murder with political fanaticism, Burdett's speeches &c. &c. C.L. was apparently affected but could not help mingling with humour his real concern at the event, for he talked of loving his Regent.

C. said to me in a half whisper that W.'s letter had been perfectly satisfactory to him & that he had answered it immediately. I flatter myself therefore that my pains will not have been lost & that through the interchange of statements wh. but for me wd. probably never have been made, a reconciliation will have taken place most desirable & salutary.

16th. Sent Mrs. Clarkson a letter giving an account of the reconciliation of W. & C. . . .

19. . . . Wordsworth called on me about 12 o'c. . . . W. has seen C. several times & been much in his company but they have not yet touched upon the subject of their correspondence. Thus, as I hoped, the wound is healed, but, as I observed to Mrs. C[larkson], probably the scar remains in Coleridge's bosom. . . .

B.—LETTERS

CRABB ROBINSON *to* THOMAS ROBINSON.

20th May 1812

You have I suppose heard from Mrs. Clarkson that Wordsw. is in town. His being here has contributed too

much to distract my mind from what [ought] to be its sole
object of pursuit ; but to shun such a man as W. or neglect
to seize every occasion of being in his company is beyond
my power. I have likewise had an occasion to see him in
an interesting situation. I found that he & C. had no
common friend to interfere & by merely being the bearer
of civil messages & explanatory letters heal the breach wh.
has subsisted between them. And I therefore undertook
the task & I rejoice to say with success. But do not speak
of it. I wrote an account. of the negociation to Mrs.
Clarkson, because she was privy to the rupture, & was
entitled to know the event, but I do not for obvious reasons
mention my concern in the reconciliation. That two *such
men* as W. & C. (one I believe the greatest man now living
in this country & the other a man of astonishing genius &
talents tho' not harmoniously blended as in his happier
friend to form a great & good man) shd. have their relation
towards each other affected by anythg. such a being as I cd.
do seems strange & I do not wish to have the thought
excited, certainly not by my own uncalled for mention of
the transaction. There is no affected humility in this
remark. . . .

W. without saying a complimentary thing to me has
done what really flattered me, has offered to go & visit
any one of my friends to whom I wish to introduce
him. . . .

Coleridge began his course of lectures at Willis's Rooms
on Tuesday. He very obligingly gave me a ticket for
myself *& friends*. . .

MRS. CLARKSON *to* CRABB ROBINSON.

[P.M. *May* 29. 1812.]
My dear friend !
I am very much obliged to you for your letter. I shall
not revert to it further than to say that I am pleased that

COLERIDGE AND WORDSWORTH

W. & C. are likely to come together. For my own part, the whole affair must be the cause of lasting regret to me—but that signifies nothing. I knew before that C. was worthless as a friend—but nothing would have made me believe that he, who knew W. so thoroughly & who must know himself could have acted as he has by W. . . .

APPENDIX

BLAKE AUTOGRAPH

BEING EXTRACTS FROM WORDSWORTH'S
PREFACE TO *THE EXCURSION* AND FROM *THE RECLUSE* COPIED WITH THE ANNOTATIONS
HERE GIVEN [1]

It is not the Author's intention formally to announce a System. It was more animating to him to proceed on a different course & if he shall succeed in conveying to the Mind clear thoughts, lively images & strong feelings, the Reader will have no difficulty in extracting the system for himself. And in the meantime the following passage, taken from the conclusion of the first book of the Recluse may be acceptable as a Prospectus of the design of the scope of the whole Poem. [Wordsworth.]

> On Man, on Nature, and on Human Life,
> Musing in solitude, I oft perceive
> Fair trains of imagery before me rise,
> Accompanied by feelings of delight,
> Pure, or with no unpleasing sadness mixed ;
> And I am conscious of affecting thoughts
> And dear remembrances, whose presence soothes
> Or elevates the Mind, intent to weigh
> The good and evil of our mortal state.
> —To these emotions, whencesoe'er they come,
> Whether from breath of outward circumstance,
> Or from the Soul—an impulse to herself—
> I would give utterance in numerous verse.
> Of Truth, of Grandeur, Beauty, Love, and Hope,
> And melancholy Fear subdued by Faith ;

---

[1] [Cf. *ante*, pp. 5, 11, and 15. The Blake autograph is preserved at the end of the last volume of H. Crabb Robinson's Correspondence (1864–67) in Dr. Williams's Library.]

APPENDIX

Of blessed consolations in distress ;
Of moral strength and intellectual Power ;
Of joy in widest commonalty spread ;
Of the individual Mind that keeps her own
Inviolate retirement, subject there
To Conscience only, and the law supreme
Of that Intelligence which governs all—
I sing : " fit audience let me find though few ! "
So prayed, more gaining than he asked, the Bard—
In holiest mood. Urania, I shall need
Thy guidance, or a greater Muse, if such
Descend to earth or dwell in highest heaven !
For I must tread on shadowy ground, must sink
Deep—and, aloft descending, breathe in worlds
To which the heaven of heavens is but a veil.
All strength—all terror, single or in bands,
That ever was put forth in personal form—
Jehovah—with his thunder, and the choir
Of shouting Angels, and the empyreal thrones—
I pass them unalarmed.[1] Not Chaos, not
The darkest pit of lowest Erebus,
Nor aught of blinder vacancy, scooped out
By help of dreams—can breed such fear and awe
As fall upon us often when we look
Into our Minds, into the Mind of Man—
My haunt, and the main region of my song
—Beauty—a living Presence of the earth,
Surpassing the most fair ideal Forms
Which craft of delicate Spirits hath composed
From earth's materials—waits upon my steps ;
Pitches her tents before me as I move,
An hourly neighbour. Paradise, and groves
Elysian, Fortunate Fields—like those of old
Sought in the Atlantic Main—why should they be

[1] [Cf. *ante*, p. 5.]
160

APPENDIX

A history only of departed things,
Or a mere fiction of what never was ?
For the discerning intellect of Man,
When wedded to this goodly universe
In love and holy passion, shall find these
A simple produce of the common day.
—I, long before the blissful hour arrives,
Would chant, in lonely peace, the spousal verse
Of this great consummation—and, by words
Which speak of nothing more than what we are,
Would I arouse the sensual from their sleep
Of Death, and win the vacant and the vain
To noble raptures ; while my voice proclaims
How exquisitely the individual Mind
(And the progressive powers perhaps no less
Of the whole species) to the external World
Is fitted—and how exquisitely, too—[1]
Theme this but little heard of among men—
The external World is fitted to the Mind ;
And the creation (by no lower name
Can it be called) which they with blended might
Accomplish—this is our high argument.
—Such grateful haunts foregoing, if I oft
Must turn elsewhere—to travel near the tribes
And fellowships of men, and see ill sights
Of madding passions mutually inflamed ;
Must *hear Humanity in fields and groves* [2]
Pipe solitary anguish ; or must hang

---

[1] You shall not bring me down to believe such fitting &
fitted. I know better & please your Lordship. [Blake.]
[2] Does not this Fit and is it not Fitting most Exquisitely too
but to what—not to Mind but to the Vile Body only & to its
Laws of Good & Evil & its Enmities against Mind. [Blake.]
[Blake is responsible for the italics in the text.]

APPENDIX

Brooding above the fierce confederate storm
Of sorrow, barricaded evermore
Within the walls of cities—may these sounds
Have their authentic comment ; that even these
Hearing, I be not downcast or forlorn !—
Descend, prophetic Spirit ! that inspir'st
The human Soul of universal earth,
Dreaming on things to come : and dost possess
A metropolitan temple in the hearts
Of mighty Poets ; upon me bestow
A gift of genuine insight ; that my Song
With star-like virtue in its place may shine,
Shedding benignant influence, and secure
Itself from all malevolent effect
Of those mutations that extend their sway
Throughout the nether sphere !—And if with this
I mix more lowly matter ; with the thing
Contemplated, describe the Mind and Man
Contemplating ; and who, and what he was—
The transitory Being that beheld
This Vision—when and where, and how he lived ;
Be not this labour useless. If such theme
May sort with highest objects, then—dread Power !
Whose gracious favour is the primal source
Of all illumination—may my life
Express the image of a better time,
More wise desires, and simpler manners ;—nurse
My Heart in genuine freedom :—all pure thoughts
Be with me ;—so shall thy unfailing love
Guide, and support, and cheer me to the end !

[WORDSWORTH].

Solomon when he married Pharaoh's daughter &
became a convert to the Heathen Mythology talked
exactly in this way of Jehovah as a very inferior object of
man's contemplation. He also passed him by unalarmed &

APPENDIX

was permitted   Jehovah dropped a tear and followed him
by his Spirit into the Abstract Void. It is called the Divine
Mercy. Satan dwells in it, but Mercy does not dwell in
him. He knows not to forgive. [Signed] W. Blake.

INDEX

INDEX

INDEX

INDEX

INDEX

169

INDEX

170

INDEX

INDEX

INDEX

INDEX

INDEX

INDEX

Printed in England at the Cloister Press, Heaton Mersey, nr. Manchester

BIBLIOLIFE

Old Books Deserve a New Life
www.bibliolife.com

Did you know that you can get most of our titles in our trademark **EasyScript**™ print format? **EasyScript**™ provides readers with a larger than average typeface, for a reading experience that's easier on the eyes.

Did you know that we have an ever-growing collection of books in many languages?

Order online:
www.bibliolife.com/store

Or to exclusively browse our **EasyScript**™ collection:
www.bibliogrande.com

At BiblioLife, we aim to make knowledge more accessible by making thousands of titles available to you – quickly and affordably.

Contact us:
BiblioLife
PO Box 21206
Charleston, SC 29413

CPSIA information can be obtained
at www.ICGtesting.com
Printed in the USA
BVHW080821090919
557927BV00016B/349/P

9 781110 073726